The Goodison Park Encyclopedia

THE
GOODISON PARK
ENCYCLOPEDIA

An A-Z of Everton FC

Dean Hayes

MAINSTREAM
PUBLISHING

EDINBURGH AND LONDON

First published in Great Britain in 1998 by
MAINSTREAM PUBLISHING COMPANY (EDINBURGH) LTD
7 Albany Street
Edinburgh EH1 3UG

ISBN 1 84018 042 0

A catalogue record for this book is available from the British Library

Typeset in Janson Text
Printed and bound in Great Britain by The Cromwell Press Ltd

A

ABANDONED MATCHES. Early in 1905, a tremendous winning run of six consecutive games took Everton to the top of the first division. They faced Woolwich Arsenal in a crucial game at Plumstead. The match was a rearranged fixture, the first game having been called off when the Blues were leading 3–1 with just 15 minutes remaining. The inevitable happened and Everton lost 2–1. Newcastle United leapt into the top spot and won their last game to clinch the championship.

ABBOTT, WALTER. After scoring 33 goals for Small Heath in 1898–99, Walter Abbott joined Everton in the summer of 1899 and made his debut in the opening match of the following season, a 2–1 defeat at home to Sheffield United. At Small Heath, he had played inside-forward but at Everton he was switched to left-half and went on to play in 291 league and Cup games for the Blues, scoring 37 goals. Surprisingly, Abbott's only England cap was at centre-half. He played in a goalless draw against Wales at Wrexham in 1902. He also played in the club's FA Cup final appearances in 1906 and 1907, picking up a winners' medal in the first of those finals when Everton beat Newcastle United 1–0. He left Goodison in the close season of 1908 and joined Burnley before returning to play for Small Heath, by then renamed Birmingham, now Birmingham City.

ABLETT, GARY. Liverpool born and bred, Gary Ablett joined the Reds but made his Football League debut for Derby County while on loan, at home to Bournemouth in January 1985. He gained further league experience on loan to Hull City before playing his first league match for Liverpool in December 1986. He soon established a regular place in the Liverpool team and was a member of the side that beat Everton 3–2 in the FA Cup final of 1989. He won two league championship medals with Liverpool but after appearing in 147 first-team games he left Anfield to join Everton for a fee of £750,000. He settled down well at Goodison Park, playing both at left-back and in central defence. He continued to produce excellent displays despite the change of personnel when injuries decimated the back four, but with increased competition, he lost his place midway through the 1995–96 season and went on loan to Sheffield United. Though the Blades tried to sign him on a permanent basis, it was Birmingham City who secured his services for £400,000 in June 1996 after he had appeared in 156 games for Everton.

AGGREGATE SCORES. Everton's highest aggregate score in any competition came in the Football League Cup second-round match against Wrexham in 1990–91 when they notched up 11 goals over two legs. The Blues won the first leg at the Racecourse Ground 5–0 with Tony Cottee scoring a hat-trick and then won 6–0 at Goodison Park with Graeme Sharp finding the net three times.

Daniel Amokachi

AMOKACHI, DANIEL. Top scorer for Nigeria in the 1994 World Cup with two goals, Daniel Amokachi moved into the Premiership from FC Bruges in August 1994 for what was then a club record fee of £3 million. He became the first black player for nearly two decades to wear the royal blue of Everton when he made his debut in a 3–0 defeat at Blackburn. He scored on his home debut, a 2–2 draw against Queens Park Rangers. One of his greatest days for the Blues came in the FA Cup semi-final of 1995 when he came off the bench to inspire the club to a 4–1 win over Tottenham Hotspur, scoring twice in the last eight minutes. In the final against Manchester United, Amokachi was again a substitute, this time coming on for Anders Limpar and becoming the first Nigerian ever to win an FA Cup winners' medal. The lightning-fast striker who combines speed and strength with a variety of skills left the club in July 1996 to join Besiktas of Turkey for £1.75 million.

APPEARANCES. Neville Southall holds the record for the greatest number of appearances in an Everton side, with a total of 747 games to his credit between 1981 and 1997. In all, Southall has played 566 league games, 70 FA Cup games, 64 Football League Cup games and 37 other matches including European games. The players with the highest number of appearances are:

	League	*FA Cup*	*League Cup*	*Others*	*Total*
Neville Southall	566	70	64	37	747
Brian Labone	451	45	15	22	533
Ted Sagar	463	32	0	2	497
Kevin Ratcliffe	356(3)	58	46	30(1)	490(4)
Dave Watson	367(2)	44	35	16(1)	462(3)
Jack Taylor	400	56	0	0	456
Peter Farrell	422	31	0	0	453
Mick Lyons	364(25)	29(1)	34	9	436(26)
Dixie Dean	399	32	0	2	433
Tommy Eglington	394	34	0	0	428

ARRIDGE, SMART. A full-back who could play on either flank, Smart Arridge began his career with Welsh club Bangor. The tough-tackling defender renowned for his shoulder charges soon attracted the attention of the leading clubs of the day and in 1892 he joined second division Bootle. Everton persuaded him to join them but, even though he signed for the Goodison club in 1893, he had to wait until 1895–96 before establishing himself as a first-team regular. Although Arridge was born in Sunderland, his Welsh boyhood was a good enough qualification for him to be selected for that country, and during his time with Everton he won three full international caps. When Everton reached the FA Cup final in 1897, Arridge had played in the first three rounds and was rather surprisingly omitted from the semi-final and final line-ups. Bitterly disappointed, he left Goodison in the close season to play for New Brighton Tower.

ATTENDANCES – AVERAGE. Everton's average home league attendances over the past ten seasons have been as follows:

1988–89	27,786	1993–94	22,876
1989–90	26,280	1994–95	31,367
1990–91	25,028	1995–96	35,435
1991–92	23,148	1996–97	36,186
1992–93	20,445	1997–98	35,376

ATTENDANCE – HIGHEST. The record attendance at Goodison Park is 78,299 for the first division game against Liverpool on 18 September 1948. For the record, the game finished 1–1 with Ephraim Dodds scoring for the Toffees.

ATTENDANCE – LOWEST. The lowest attendance at Goodison Park for a competitive game involving the club's first team was on 23 February 1899 when a crowd of 2,079 saw Everton lose 1–0 to West Bromwich Albion.

AWAY MATCHES. Everton's best away wins came in a second division match at Charlton Athletic on 7 February 1931 when they won 7–0, and in three matches against Derby County. The Toffees won 6–2 at the Baseball Ground in 1890–91, 6–1 in 1892–93 and 6–2 in 1953–54. Everton also won 6–2 at West Bromwich Albion in 1967–68. Everton's worst defeat away from home is the 10–4 beating handed out by Tottenham Hotspur on 11 October 1958.

AWAY SEASONS. The club's highest number of away wins came in seasons 1969–70 and 1984–85 when they won 12 of their 21 matches. They won the first division championship on each occasion. The most away goals scored by the club is 45 in 1930–31 when the Blues won the second division championship.

B

BAILEY, JOHN. Liverpool-born left-back John Bailey began his career with Blackburn Rovers for whom he made 120 league appearances during four seasons at Ewood Park. He joined Everton in the summer of 1979 for a fee of £300,000 and made his debut in a 4–2 home defeat by Norwich City on the opening day of the 1979–80 season. He was the club's only ever-present during that campaign as they struggled to avoid relegation. His form was such that within a year of his arrival at Goodison he had won England B international honours. A firm favourite with the Everton fans, he helped the club win the FA Cup in 1984 when they beat Watford 2–0 at Wembley. But a few months later he lost his regular full-back spot to Welsh international Pat Van Den Hauwe who joined the club from Birmingham City. He eventually left Goodison in 1985 after appearing in 220 first-team games and signed for Newcastle United for a fee of £80,000. In 1988 he left St James's Park, joining Bristol City on a free transfer before returning to Goodison as B team coach in 1992. Sadly, a year later he was dismissed.

BALL, ALAN. One of the greatest players ever to pull on an Everton shirt, Alan Ball inspired his country to World Cup success in 1966 and played a major role in the Blues' championship-winning season of 1969–70. As a boy, he was football mad but after trials with Wolves and Bolton, he was rejected by both. In the end, it was only the persistence of his footballing father, Alan Ball senior, that persuaded Blackpool to sign him. He made his first-team debut for the Seasiders against Liverpool at Anfield in 1962 at 17 years of age. Within 12 months he had become a regular in the Bloomfield Road club's side. He went on

Alan Ball

to play in 126 league and Cup games for Blackpool before joining Everton in August 1966, immediately after his scintillating contribution to England's World Cup victory. The £110,000 deal went through much to the annoyance of Don Revie who desperately wanted to sign Ball for Leeds United but was unable to persuade his board to pay what was then the highest fee to pass between British clubs. Ball made his Everton debut at Fulham in the opening match of the 1966–67 season, scoring the game's only goal. In fact, in his first two seasons with the club, he was the leading scorer and in 1967–68 when he netted 20 league goals, he scored four in a 6–2 win at West Bromwich Albion. With Colin Harvey and Howard Kendall, he was part of the celebrated midfield trio which swept Everton to the title in 1969–70. For no apparent reason, that side broke up within a couple of years and when Harry Catterick was asked to put a value on Ball's head, he said he would expect offers in the region of £1 million. When asked if he would ever part company with his prized asset, he replied, 'I'd consider it and then I'd say no.' Imagine then the utter consternation when Ball left for Arsenal for £220,000 some nine months later, after scoring 78 goals in 249 league and Cup games for the Goodison club. After a successful career at Highbury, Ball moved to Southampton for £60,000 in March 1976, then to Blackpool as manager in 1980. He resigned in March 1981 and returned to Southampton, playing his last game in the top flight in October 1982. After a short spell in Hong Kong, he resumed his playing career with Bristol Rovers before managing Portsmouth, whom he took into the first division. In 1989 he left to manage Stoke City but was dismissed two years later following a string of poor results. He later managed Exeter City, Southampton and Manchester City, but has now returned to Fratton Park to take charge of Portsmouth for a second time.

BALMER, ROBERT. The younger brother of Walter Balmer, Robert made his debut for Everton in the 3–0 win over Middlesbrough at Goodison Park on 3 January 1903, but it was another three seasons before he became a regular member of the side. Forming an effective full-back partnership with his brother, they appeared together on 64 occasions including the 1907 FA Cup final against Sheffield Wednesday at the Crystal Palace. When Walter joined Croydon Common, Robert formed another good full-back partnership with John Maconnachie and went on to make 188 league and Cup appearances before hanging up his boots.

BALMER, WALTER. A tough-tackling full-back, Walter Balmer could play on either flank and after making his debut in a 2–2 draw at West Bromwich Albion in November 1897 he established himself as a first-team regular. Forming a good partnership with Jack Crelley, he went on to play in 331 league and Cup games for the club, winning an FA Cup winners' medal in 1906, the Blues beating Newcastle United 1–0 in the final. A year earlier he won his only England cap when he played against Ireland at Middlesbrough. He partnered his younger brother Robert on a number of occasions including the FA Cup final of 1907 when they lost 2–1 to Sheffield Wednesday. He also represented the Football League but at the end of the 1907–8 season he was allowed to leave Goodison and joined Southern League Croydon Common. After the First World War, he joined Huddersfield Town as coach.

BARMBY, NICK. The son of the old Hull City player, Jeff Barmby, Nick attended the FA's national school at Lilleshall before joining Tottenham Hotspur in March 1990. He made his competitive debut against

Sheffield Wednesday in September 1992; coming on as a substitute against Middlesbrough in his first home game, he scored a late equaliser. He became the focus of a club-versus-country row when he was selected for the England Youth side to compete in the World Cup finals in Australia. Even though Tottenham wanted him to stay and help them during their FA Cup campaign, the FA got their way and he went to Australia. After helping England to third place, he returned to Spurs for their losing FA Cup semi-final against Arsenal. In the summer of 1995, he was surprisingly allowed to leave White Hart Lane and joined Premier League new boys Middlesbrough for £5.25 million. He scored on his debut for the Riverside club against Arsenal and quickly established himself as a firm favourite at the new Holgate end with his exciting midfield displays. After scoring a hat-trick against China, he was included in the national squad for Euro '96. Barmby joined Everton in October 1996 for a fee of £5.75 million and, apart from the odd flashes of brilliance, he has been beset by poor form. Nevertheless, he remains an important member of the Everton squad.

BARRETT, EARL. Although Earl Barrett began his career as an apprentice with Manchester City, he made his Football League debut whilst on loan with Chester City at Mansfield Town in March 1986. He made his City debut at home to Luton Town two months later. He did not make progress at Maine Road and in November 1987 he joined Oldham Athletic for £35,000. In 1989–90, he was ever present; the club were losing League Cup finalists and progressed to the semi-final of the FA Cup. The following season he hardly put a foot wrong, again playing in every game as the Boundary Park club won the second division title. He was rewarded for his fine displays at club level when he was chosen for England's tour of Australasia in the summer of 1991. In February 1992 he joined Aston Villa for a fee of £1.7 million and the following season he was a key player as the club ended the campaign runners-up to Manchester United. He went on to appear in 150 first-team games for Villa before joining Everton, also for £1.7 million, in January 1995. He made his debut in a 2–0 defeat at Newcastle United two days after signing and, though his time at Goodison has been hampered by injuries, he has proved adept enough to slot in either at centre-back or right-back.

BEAGRIE, PETER. After making his league debut for his home-town club Middlesbrough, Peter Beagrie joined Sheffield United prior to the start of the 1986–87 season. He established himself as joint leading goalscorer with nine to his credit that term, and won his first and only international honours, at Under-21 level. Following the Blades' relegation to the third division, he was transferred to Stoke City for £210,000. His displays for the Potters attracted the attention of several top-flight clubs and in November 1989, he joined Everton for a fee of £750,000. He made his debut as a substitute in a 6–2 defeat at Aston Villa but he failed to perform with any consistency during his first two seasons at Goodison and was in and out of the side. When he was loaned to Sunderland early in the 1991–92 season, a permanent transfer out of Goodison seemed likely. However, he was recalled and reinstated and, though he was frequently relegated to substitute, he went on to play in 132 league and Cup games before being transferred to Manchester City for £1.1 million in March 1994. A highly skilled traditional winger, Peter Beagrie has been hampered at Maine Road by a series of injury problems.

BEARDSLEY, PETER. One of the most gifted players of his generation, Peter Beardsley made his Football League debut for Carlisle United at home to Blackburn Rovers in August 1979. He spent three years at Brunton Park before trying his luck in North America with Vancouver Whitecaps. His success in Canada alerted Manchester United and they brought him back to Britain, but within six months he was back in Vancouver without playing a single league game for the Old Trafford club. A year later, Newcastle United signed him and in 1983–84, his first season with the club, he scored 20 goals as the Magpies won promotion to the first division. After ending the next two seasons as the club's top scorer, it came as a great shock to the Geordie faithful when he was allowed to join Liverpool for £1.9 million. He won a league championship medal in his first season at Anfield, which was followed by an FA Cup winners' medal in 1989 and another league title triumph in 1989–90. Beardsley was more a creator than scorer of goals, although in 1990–91 he netted 11 goals in his first 11 games, including a hat-trick against Manchester United. After losing his place through injury, he was surprisingly ignored by manager Kenny Dalglish when he had regained full fitness. He was reinstated after Dalglish's sudden departure, and it came as a shock when new manager Graeme Souness allowed him to join Everton in the summer of 1991. After failing to score in his first six games, Beardsley found the target eight times in his next six outings and ended the season as the club's top scorer. He was the mainstay of the Everton side during two disappointing seasons, but with the club desperately needing money to rebuild the team he was sold to Newcastle United for £1.4 million during the 1993 close season. He scored 118 goals in 319 games in his two spells at St James's

Park. Early in the 1997–98 season, he joined newly promoted Premier League side Bolton Wanderers for £500,000, but is now on loan at Fulham.

BELL, JOHN. Scottish international forward John Bell was a member of Dumbarton's Scottish League championship winning side of 1891–92 before signing for Everton. He spent the best part of a decade entertaining the Everton crowd. In 1897, when the Blues lost 3–2 to Aston Villa in the FA Cup final, his outstanding performance nearly swung the game Everton's way. In 1894–95 he was the club's leading scorer with 15 goals in 27 games and in that season's FA Cup competition, he scored his first hat-trick as the Blues lost 4–3 at Aston Villa. He topped the club's goalscoring charts again in 1896–97, repeating the feat of two seasons earlier, scoring 15 goals in 27 league games. Three of his goals came in the 6–3 win over West Bromwich Albion on 17 April 1897. At the end of the following season, he left Everton to play for Spurs, Glasgow Celtic and New Brighton Tower before returning to Goodison for the 1901–2 season. In the summer of 1903 he joined Preston North End as player-coach and was chairman of the first attempt at a players' union.

BENTHAM, STANLEY. Leigh-born Stanley Bentham had a number of trials with his local club, Bolton Wanderers, but, failing to secure a contract, he turned professional with non-league Wigan Athletic. After a series of impressive performances for the Latics, he found himself the target of several first division clubs and in February 1934, he joined Everton, along with team-mate Terry Kavanagh. He had to wait until November 1935 before making his first-team debut, but it was well worth waiting for – he scored two goals in the club's first away success of the season, a 4–0 win at Grimsby Town. When Everton won the first division championship in 1938–39, he missed only one match – a 7–0 defeat at Wolverhampton Wanderers – and scored his only hat-trick for the club in a 6–2 home win over Sunderland. He continued to play for Everton throughout the war. In all, he appeared in 216 matches, playing the last of his 125 league and Cup games in December 1948. He then joined the Everton backroom staff, occupying a variety of roles until he left Goodison in 1962 to take up a coaching post with Luton Town.

BERNARD, MIKE. An aggressive tackling midfielder who could also play at full-back, Mike Bernard began his career with Stoke City. While he was there, he won three England Under-23 caps and helped the Potters to win the League Cup in 1972. Soon after that triumph however, Stoke manager Tony Waddington sold him to Everton for £140,000. Although hampered by injuries during his five seasons at Goodison Park, Bernard played in 171 league and Cup games and was an important member of the Everton squad that finished runners-up in the League Cup in 1976–77. There was talk of a return to the Victoria Ground, but he eventually joined Oldham Athletic. Unfortunately, he suffered a bad calf injury and after just six appearances for the Boundary Park club he was forced to quit the game.

BEST START. Everton were unbeaten for the first 19 games of the 1978–79 first division season when they finished fourth. They won eleven and drew eight of those matches before losing 3–2 at Coventry City on 23 December. In 1894–95, when the club ended the season as runners-up in the first division, they won their first eight games of the season.

BIGGEST DEFEATS. The club's biggest defeat in the Football League occurred on 11 October 1958 when they lost 10–4 to Tottenham Hotspur at White Hart Lane. Everton have also lost three matches by a 7–0 scoreline – to Sunderland on 26 December 1934, Wolverhampton Wanderers on 22 February 1939 and Portsmouth on 10 September 1949. The club's worst home defeat was the 7–3 scoreline inflicted on the club by Newcastle United on 26 December 1933.

BIGGEST WINS. The club's biggest win in the FA Cup is 11–2 over Derby County on 18 January 1890. In the Football League, both Manchester City (3 September 1906) and Plymouth Argyle (27 December 1930) have been beaten 9–1 whilst Stoke (2 November 1889) and Southampton (20 November 1971) have been defeated 8–0. Everton scored nine goals on two occasions during the 1931–32 season, beating Sheffield Wednesday 9–3 and Leicester City 9–2.

BILIC, SLAVEN. Outstanding Croatian international Slaven Bilic formed part of the backbone of the team which reached the quarter-final of Euro '96 and has now won more than 30 caps for his country. He joined West Ham United from Karlsruhe in Germany in February 1996 for £1.3 million and almost single-handedly shored up the Hammers' defence, with his fierce tackling and heading ability quickly becoming evident. Bilic became the world's most expensive defender when Everton paid West Ham £4.5 million for him in May 1997. The move to Goodison had been on the cards for a number of months since Everton discovered a clause in his contract which revealed that any club offering more than £4 million was entitled to negotiate personal terms with the 28-year-old defender, who has a law degree. The Blues snapped him up on a five-year contract and he made his league debut in a goalless draw at Bolton's new Reebok Stadium. Injuries and suspensions marred his first season with the club but 'Super Slav' is sure to prove a big bargain.

Billy Bingham

BINGHAM, BILLY. Billy Bingham started his illustrious career with Irish League club Glentoran. Sunderland introduced him to English football in 1951. Within two years of his arrival at Roker Park, he was a permanent member of the Northern Ireland team. All told, he won 56 caps, equalling Danny Blanchflower's record, later beaten by Terry Neill. Bingham was a superb dribbler and crosser of the ball, revelling in one-to-one situations. The highlight of his international career was being part of the Irish team to reach the World Cup quarter-finals in

Sweden in 1958. He played in over 200 league and Cup games for Sunderland before joining Luton Town for £15,000 during the summer of 1958. He arrived at Goodison in October 1960 and made his Everton debut in a 3–2 win at Fulham. He scored 26 goals in 98 first-team games for Everton, winning a league championship medal in 1962–63 before leaving for Port Vale, where a broken leg brought his playing days to an end. He became manager of Southport, leading them to promotion for the first time in their history. After spells at Plymouth and Linfield, he took charge of the Greek national side before returning to Goodison as manager in May 1973. Don Revie, Jimmy Armfield and Bobby Robson had all turned the Everton job down and Bingham inherited a team badly in need of major reconstruction. Bingham, a likeable man with a keen sense of humour, took the club to seventh spot in the first division – a huge improvement on the previous two seasons. He smashed the British transfer record when he signed Bob Latchford from Birmingham City for £350,000. In 1974–75, the club came fourth in the first division but in January 1977 with the Blues in 13th place, Bingham was sacked. He later took charge at Mansfield Town and led the Northern Ireland team to the World Cup finals in 1982 and 1986.

BOOKS. The many books that have been written about Everton Football Club include:

Everton: The Official Centenary History, John Roberts
Everton Football Club, Ric George
Everton: A Complete Record, Ian Ross and Gordon Smailes
Forever Everton, Stephen F. Kelly
Everton, Matthew Graham

BOOTH, TOM. Having played his early football with Holley Hill and Ashton North End, Tom Booth was chosen to play for the Rest of Lancashire against Nelson in 1896, and such was his form that Blackburn Rovers had no hesitation in securing his signature. Moving from wing-half to centre-half, Booth was capped by England, appearing in the 3–0 win over Wales at Wrexham on 28 March 1898. He left Ewood Park in April 1900 – Rovers needed the cash – and joined Everton. He played his first match for the club in a 2–1 win at Preston North End on the opening day of the 1900–1 season and soon established himself in the side. At the end of the season he was made captain and in 1901–2, when he was ever present, he led the club to runners-up spot in the first division. The Blues were also runners-up in

1904–5 and finished third in 1903–4 and 1906–7. When Everton reached the 1906 FA Cup final, Booth was injured and had to sit out the match; 12 months later, when the club again won through to the final, there was no room for him. He left Goodison in 1908 for Preston North End but left Deepdale for Carlisle United without having played a league game for the Lilywhites.

BOYES, WALLY. A schoolboy prodigy, diminutive winger Wally Boyes once scored 17 goals in a game as his side won 31–2, yet even then he showed his great enthusiasm for the game when he demanded a late penalty! Standing only 5ft 3ins, with one leg shorter than the other, he joined Everton from West Bromwich Albion in 1938. He had scored the first goal for the Hawthorns club in the 1935 FA Cup final against Sheffield Wednesday and overall hit 35 goals in 151 games for Albion. Boyes made his debut for the Blues in a thrilling 4–4 draw at Leeds United, having a hand in all the goals. In 1938 he was capped twice by England, against Wales and the Rest of Europe. His progress was interrupted by the Second World War, but he appeared in 121 wartime games before resuming his league career at Goodison in 1946–47. He went on to score 15 goals in 73 league and Cup games before playing for Notts County and later Scunthorpe United. Boyes was also player-manager of Retford, manager of Hyde United and trainer to Swansea Town.

BOYLE, RICHARD. Another of the club's Scottish imports, Richard Boyle played his early football with Dumbarton Episcopalians, Dumbarton Union and Dumbarton before joining Everton in 1890. The strong-tackling half-back made an immediate impact on the English game and in only his second season with the club was made captain. Boyle rarely missed a game in his eight seasons with the Toffees and was ever present in seasons 1894–95, 1895–96 and 1898–99. Renowned for his pin-point passing, Boyle loved nothing more than to surge forward out of defence to help the attack. Deadly from free-kicks, Boyle scored some very important goals for Everton during his 243 appearances, the last of which came in a 1–1 draw at Wolverhampton Wanderers in January 1901.

BRACEWELL, PAUL. A superb passer of the ball, Paul Bracewell played for Stoke City for three full seasons before following manager Alan Durban to Sunderland for £250,000. Things didn't work out for him at Roker Park and after just one season he moved to Everton. Bracewell holds the rare distinction of making his Everton debut at Wembley, where he played in the Charity Shield showpiece against Liverpool on 18 August 1984. Forming a good understanding with Peter Reid in the Everton midfield, he won his first full England cap when he replaced Bryan Robson against West Germany on the summer tour to Mexico. On New Year's Day 1986, Bracewell suffered a serious ankle injury in a 2–2 draw at Newcastle United and was out of action for more than 20 months. During this time, he had undergone five operations and after returning to the first team towards the end of the 1987–88 season, he was forced to undergo even more surgery on his right ankle. He had appeared in 135 first-team games, winning league championship and European Cup-Winners' Cup medals, when in 1989 he rejoined Sunderland in a £250,000 transfer. He played for the Wearsiders in the 1992 FA Cup final – the fourth time he had picked up a runners-up medal – before joining Newcastle United. He made a telling contribution to the Magpies' promotion to the Premier League before, in the summer of 1995, returning to Sunderland for his third spell with the club. His experience proved vital as Sunderland went back up to the top flight as first division champions.

BREWSTER, GEORGE. Born at Culsamond near Aberdeen, centre-half George Brewster played his early football with Mugiemoss before joining Aberdeen in 1913. He was a regular in the Dons side until the outbreak of the First World War when he guested for Falkirk, returning to Pittodrie at the end of the hostilities. He joined Everton in January 1920 for a fee of £1,500 and made his debut in a 1–1 draw at home to Sheffield Wednesday. In 1920–21, he established himself as the club's first-choice centre-half, following Tom Fleetwood's switch to right-half, and was so impressive that he was capped by Scotland for the 3–0 win over England in April 1921. Yet midway through the following season, he was less sure of a first-team place and in November 1922, after playing in 68 league and Cup games, he left Everton and joined Wolverhampton Wanderers. He then played for Lovell's Athletic and Wallasey United before becoming coach to Brooklands Athletic in New York. Later, he returned to his native Scotland to become player-manager at Inverness.

BRITISH CHAMPIONSHIPS. Everton faced Glasgow Rangers in the newly created British Championship over two legs during the 1963–64 season. After winning the home leg on 27 November 1963 by 3–1 with goals from Scott, Temple and Young, Everton drew 1–1 at Ibrox to take the trophy 4–2 on aggregate with Alex Young netting the Blues' goal.

BRITTON, CLIFF. Cliff Britton was a footballing genius who was later to turn his talents to management. He arrived at Everton in 1930 after beginning his career with Bristol Rovers. Initially he was considered too lightweight to cope with the rough and tumble of a central position and was played at outside-right in the club's Central League side. He made his first-team debut for the Blues in October 1930 in a 4–2 home win over Tottenham Hotspur and never looked back. A cultured wing-half, whose passing ability was second to none, he was in the Everton side that beat Manchester City in the 1933 FA Cup final, and won the first of nine England caps against Wales in 1934. He went on to play in 240 league and Cup games for Everton, though when the Blues won the league championship in 1938–39, he played in only one game, being an adviser to the reserve squad. During the Second World War, his career enjoyed something of a revival as he won 12 wartime caps, forming a fine England half-back line with Cullis and Mercer. After the war had ended, he took charge at Burnley, leading them from the second division to third place in the top flight and to the FA Cup final. In September 1948, he was appointed manager of Everton and immediately began to introduce some stability to a side which was never really good enough to live with the leading teams of the day. He took the club to an FA Cup semi-final with Liverpool in March 1950 but the following season the club finished bottom of the first division and were relegated. However, the Everton board gave Britton a vote of confidence and in 1953–54 he took the club back into the top flight as second division runners-up. But in 1956, a dispute arose over the club wanting to appoint an acting manager while Britton was abroad with the team and so he parted company with them.

BROTHERS. Walter and Robert Balmer both played for Everton, making 64 league and Cup appearances together at full-back. Walter Balmer joined Everton in 1897 and after making his debut against West Bromwich Albion on 6 November 1897, played 331 games for the Blues. Capped by England against Ireland in 1905, he later joined Croydon Common before becoming coach at Huddersfield Town. Robert Balmer was Walter's younger brother and had the same no-nonsense style that made Everton's defence one of the best in the league. He retired in 1911 after making 188 first-team appearances. They were uncles to Jack Balmer, who was later to become one of Liverpool's most notable centre-forwards.

BROWN, SANDY. Signed from Partick Thistle for £38,000 in September 1963, Alex 'Sandy' Brown was one of the club's most versatile players. The wearer of eight different numbered outfield shirts, Brown could also play in goal and it was this versatility that led to him being named substitute in no fewer than 43 league and Cup games. When Everton entertained Leeds United in the mid-1960s, Brown was sent off in the opening minutes of a match in which the referee later had to lead both teams off the field for a cooling-down period. Though he played in four of the club's FA Cup ties in 1966, he wasn't selected for the final itself. In 1969–70, he appeared in 36 games as the Blues won the league championship. After playing in 251 league and Cup games for Everton, he left to join Shrewsbury. After a short stay at Gay Meadow, he signed for Southport and in 1972–73 was a member of their fourth division championship-winning side.

BROWN, WILLIAM. A product of the Scottish nursery, Cambuslang, William Brown did not hesitate to sign for Everton when offered a contract in the summer of 1913. He was only 17 years old when he made his Everton debut in a 4–1 win over Manchester City in December 1914 and though he lost years of his career to the First World War, he returned after the hostilities to become a member of Everton's great half-back line of the early 1920s. Recognised throughout the land for his cultured displays, he went on to appear in 179 league and Cup games before joining Nottingham Forest in May 1928. He had never scored for Everton, but at the City Ground he developed a flair for goalscoring. In August 1930, he returned to Merseyside as player-coach of Liverpool Cables FC.

BUCHAN, IAN. A one-time Scottish amateur international and former lecturer at Loughborough College, Ian Buchan was appointed team coach in succession to Cliff Britton in the summer of 1956. He was a fitness fanatic and demanded the same commitment from the Everton players. In his first game in charge, he stopped the team coach two miles short of Elland Road and made the players walk the rest of the way. Everton lost that game 5–1 and in the next three games of that 1956–57 season the side conceded ten more goals. In fact, the club let in five goals or more on five occasions during that campaign but surprisingly won 5–2 against champions Manchester United at Old Trafford. Buchan was a deep thinker and his commitment to the Goodison club was never questioned. Nevertheless, in October 1958, after he had spent just two years in the managerial chair, he parted company with the club. Sadly, he died in a motor accident in Glasgow in 1965, aged 45.

BUCKLE, TED. One of the quickest wingers ever to play for Everton, Ted Buckle joined the club from Manchester United in November 1949 and made his debut for the Blues against United less than 18 hours after completing his move from Old Trafford. That game was goalless but in the next two matches Buckle scored against Chelsea and Stoke, and in five seasons at Goodison Park the confident winger scored 33 goals in 107 appearances. Inspired by Buckle's pace, the club reached the semi-finals of the FA Cup in 1952–53 only to be beaten 4–3 by Bolton Wanderers at Maine Road. During the 1954–55 season, Buckle seemed to lose some of his speed and this, coupled with a bad knee injury, persuaded Everton to let him join Exeter City at the end of the season. He played in 65 league games for the Grecians before taking over as player-manager at Welsh League club Prestatyn.

BUCKLEY, MICK. Manchester-born Mick Buckley was a schoolboy star. Despite receiving offers to play for both City and United, he surprised everyone by opting for Everton. The aggressive midfielder worked his way through the club's ranks before making his first-team debut in a 2–2 home draw against Wolverhampton Wanderers in March 1972. He was a member of the England Youth side that won the Little World Cup in Spain in 1972 and made two appearances for the England Under-23s. He had made 156 league and Cup appearances for the Blues when he lost his place to Trevor Ross and, after a loan spell at Queens Park Rangers, he signed for Sunderland in 1978. He made an indifferent start at Roker Park but recovered to save the Wearsiders from relegation when he scored a vital goal against Manchester City in 1982. He played in 121 league games for the north-east club before moving on to Hartlepool United, Carlisle and Middlesbrough.

C

CAPACITY. The total capacity of Goodison Park in 1997-98 was 40,200.

CAPS. The most capped player in the club's history is Neville Southall who, at the time of writing, has won 91 caps for Wales.

CAPS (ENGLAND). The first Everton player to be capped by England was Johnny Holt when he played against Wales at Wrexham on 15 March 1890. Later that day, England played Ireland in Belfast with a different team altogether and Fred Geary made his debut, scoring a hat-trick in a 9–1 win. Everton's most capped England player is Alan Ball with 39 caps.

CAPS (NORTHERN IRELAND). The first Everton player to be capped by Northern Ireland was John Sheridan when he played against Wales in 1903. Everton's most capped Northern Ireland player is Billy Scott with 16 caps.

CAPS (REPUBLIC OF IRELAND). The first player to be capped by the Republic of Ireland was Tommy Eglington when he played against England in 1947. Everton's most capped Republic of Ireland player is Kevin Sheedy with 41 caps.

CAPS (SCOTLAND). The first Everton player to be capped by Scotland was John Bell when he played against England in 1896. Everton's most capped Scotland player is Graeme Sharp with 12 caps.

CAPS (WALES). The first Everton player to be capped by Wales was Joe Davies when he played against Scotland in 1889. Everton's most capped Wales player is Neville Southall with 91 caps.

CAPTAINS. Everton's first captain was Nick Ross who arrived at the club in 1888 but left after only one season following a disagreement with the board. The argument was about who should choose the team – the players and supporters demanded that Ross should have a say – there was no immediate solution, so he returned to play for Preston North End. Jimmy Galt captained the Blues when they won the league championship and reached the FA Cup semi-finals in 1914–15. He was a classic example of a player whose career was ruined by the war. Peter Farrell was a sturdy wing-half who captained the side for seven years, leading them to promotion from the second division in 1953–54. From being a schoolboy on the terraces, Brian Labone went on to captain the club and led them out at Wembley in 1966. A model professional, he led the side to two league championship titles and two FA Cup finals. At the age of 24, Kevin Ratcliffe was already the most successful captain in the history of Everton Football Club. In the 12 months between May 1984 and May 1985, he led the club forward to pick up the league championship, FA Cup, Charity Shield and the European Cup-Winners' Cup. Thereafter he skippered the Blues to runners-up in the League and FA Cup in 1985–86 and to another league title in 1986–87. He was appointed captain of Everton in December 1983 and three months later, captain of Wales.

CAREY, JOHNNY. As a player, Johnny Carey represented both Northern Ireland and the Republic within the space of four days. Perhaps the best of Matt Busby's players during Manchester United's immediate post-war glory days, Carey was so versatile that he figured in nine different positions for the Reds, ten if you include the occasion he pulled on the goalkeeper's jersey when Jack Crompton was taken ill at an away match. He led United to victory in the FA Cup final of 1948 and was voted PFA Footballer of the Year in 1949. On his retirement, Carey became manager of Blackburn Rovers and led them into the first division. This attracted the attention of Everton and, in October 1958, Carey was appointed manager of the Goodison club more than two years after Cliff Britton had departed. He took over from the club coach Ian Buchan, who had never held the title of manager. With the financial backing of John Moores, Carey went into the transfer market to sign players of the calibre of Billy Bingham, Jimmy Gabriel, Roy Vernon and Alex Young. After two disappointing seasons, Carey took

Harry Catterick

the Blues to fifth in the first division in 1960–61, their highest position since the war. At the end of that season, Carey joined Moores at the Football League AGM. In the back of a taxi, Moores told Carey that he felt the club needed a change of manager and offered him a golden handshake. Carey was, of course, stunned and saddened by events, but it was typical of the genial Irishman that he made no fuss and accepted the decision with great dignity. He later took charge at Leyton Orient and took them into the first division before ending his managerial career with five successful years at Nottingham Forest.

CATTERICK, HARRY. Harry Catterick transformed the Blues into a great footballing side once more capable of living with the best. He was appointed manager in 1961 and was given a simple brief by John Moores and that was to get Everton Football Club back to the top by means of good entertaining football. He proved very adept at wheeling and dealing in the transfer market and brought some top-class players to Goodison, including Tony Kay, Johnny Morrissey, Fred Pickering,

Gordon West and Ray Wilson. In his first season in charge, he guided the club to fourth place in the first division and, 12 months later, the revival Catterick had sparked off reached its climax as the Blues won their sixth league championship title in style. In 1966, Everton reached the FA Cup final at Wembley and Catterick's biggest gamble – the inclusion of Cornishman Mike Trebilcock – paid off; Trebilcock scored twice in a 3–2 win over Sheffield Wednesday. As his youth policy began to pay off with John Hurst, Jimmy Husband and Joe Royle all fighting their way into the first team, Catterick signed Alan Ball and a new Everton side began to take shape. In 1968 he took the club back to Wembley only for their opponents, West Bromwich Albion, to snatch the FA Cup in extra time. By the start of the 1969–70 season, Harry Catterick had built one of the finest club sides of post-war English football. The Blues swept to the league title as Ball, Harvey and Kendall ran midfield, but within a year the club had slumped to 14th place with the Everton manager unable to explain why his side had run out of confidence. In January 1972, while driving home from Sheffield, he had a heart attack. In April 1973, with four years of his contract still to run, the club moved him sideways into a senior executive role. Sadly, the man who restored pride to this famous club died at Goodison Park after an FA Cup quarter-final match against Ipswich Town in March 1985.

CENTURIES. Six players have scored 100 or more league goals for the Toffees. Dixie Dean is the greatest goalscorer with 349 strikes in his Everton career (1925–37). Other centurions are Graeme Sharp (111), Alex Young (110), Bob Latchford (106), Joe Royle (102) and Roy Vernon (101). Whilst only Jack Taylor has made over 100 consecutive league appearances for the club immediately following his debut – 122, in fact – four players have made over 100 consecutive league appearances during their careers. They are Neville Southall (212), Cyril Lello (141), Joe Royle (108) and Alec Troup (100).

CHADWICK, EDGAR. Blackburn-born Edgar Chadwick began his career with Blackburn Olympic and had one season with Blackburn Rovers before signing for Everton in the summer of 1888. He made his debut for the Blues in their opening game in the Football League against Accrington and was the club's only ever-present that season. In fact, Chadwick was an ever-present in the club's first three seasons in the Football League and made 93 consecutive league and Cup appearances from his debut before missing a game. Forming an outstanding left-wing partnership with Alf Milward, Chadwick went on to score 110 goals in 300 league and Cup games for the Blues including three hat-tricks – Burnley (home 7–3 in 1890–91), Sunderland (home 7–1 in 1893–94) and Sheffield United (home 5–0 in 1895–96). With Everton he won a league championship medal in 1890–91 and was on the losing side in two FA Cup finals in 1893 and 1897. Later, when he played for Southampton, he won a Southern League championship medal in 1900–1 and a runners-up medal in the FA Cup final of 1902. He was capped seven times by England and in the match against Scotland in 1892 scored after just 30 seconds in England's 4–1 win. He also represented the Football League and the Football Alliance and was reputed to be the first Englishman to coach abroad when he worked with teams in Germany and Holland.

CHAIRMEN. In 1988–89, Everton chairman Philip Carter became the first Football League president to be voted out of office because of the bias he and Arsenal's David Dein had supposedly shown in the negotiations with television. Carter was replaced by Jack Dunnett, the first man to hold the post twice. The club's present chairman is Peter Johnson, a multi-millionaire food magnate who has seen off three managers and three tense campaigns to avoid relegation. Mike Walker, appointed before Johnson's arrival, was axed for the worst start to a season in the club's history. Joe Royle was sacked in March 1997 when he clashed with the chairman over deadline-day signings. Johnson hardly expected plain sailing when he won the takeover battle against impresario Bill Kenwright, but at the moment he appears to have spent over £20 million, with only the FA Cup final success of 1995 to show for it. The former £3-a-week butcher's boy whose Park Food Group dominates the lucrative Christmas hamper market, is now one of the richest 150 men in Britain. Football success, however, is proving rather more elusive for the ambitious chairman who supported Liverpool and rescued Tranmere Rovers.

CHAMPIONSHIPS. Everton have won the league championship on nine occasions. The first was in 1890–91 when they took a particular liking to Derby County, who the previous season they had beaten 11–2 in the FA Cup, scoring 13 goals against the Rams in their two matches. Everton appeared to be in trouble when they lost their final fixture by a single goal at Sunderland. Luck, however, was on their side as news came through that their main rivals, Preston, had lost and Everton were champions by two points. In 1914–15, Everton beat Liverpool 5–0 at Anfield with Bobby Parker grabbing a hat-trick. Parker scored 36 goals including six hat-tricks in 35 games, equalling

Bertie Freeman's first division record. As the club went into the final game, they were on top, a point ahead of Oldham Athletic but having played one more match. While the Blues drew at home to Chelsea, Oldham lost 2–0 to Liverpool and Everton were champions for a second time. Everton won the title for a third time in 1927–28 with Dixie Dean scoring 60 goals in 39 league games. Although they were relegated for the first time in their history in 1929–30 they bounced straight back into the top flight as second division champions. They were league champions again in 1931–32, enjoying a run of ten undefeated games and pipping the great Arsenal side by two points. Dixie Dean scored five goals against both Chelsea and Sheffield Wednesday and four against Leicester City to finish with a total of 44. In 1938–39, the Blues won their first six games of the season with Tommy Lawton scoring in each and though the team picked up only three points from their final four matches, the championship was won with four points to spare. The 1962–63 season was the season of the big freeze and it was, in essence, played in two halves. The club were labelled the 'chequebook champions' because of the number of players that Harry Catterick had bought. Their strength in depth enabled them to see off the challenge of Tottenham Hotspur, Burnley and Leicester City with games to spare. They beat Spurs 1–0 to regain the leadership of the first division and then beat Fulham 4–1 in their last game of the season. This meant that the White Hart Lane club, who still had two games to play, could not overhaul them. A tremendous start and a glorious finish to the 1969–70 season meant the Blues won the championship with a nine-point margin from the reigning champions, Leeds United. The team dropped only one point in the opening seven games and finished with an unbeaten run of 14 matches. In 1984–85, the Blues clinched the league title for the eighth time by beating Queens Park Rangers 2–0 with five games still to play. The club started badly, losing their opening two games, but enjoyed a run of 18 games without defeat from Boxing Day to 8 May during which only two points were dropped. The club created the largest championship-winning margin in the first division following the introduction of three points for a win, finishing 13 points ahead of Liverpool. Everton won the league championship for the second time in three years in 1986–87, yet again at a canter – nine points ahead of Liverpool. Of their last 29 league matches, only four were lost, the club moving slowly from mid-table to the front. Howard Kendall had admirably proved the old adage that the league championship race is a marathon, not a sprint.

CHARITY SHIELD. Everton have appeared in the FA Charity Shield on 11 occasions, winning the trophy eight times. The club's record in the competition is as follows:

1928	v Blackburn Rovers (Old Trafford)	2–1
1932	v Newcastle United (St James's Park)	5–3 *
1933	v Arsenal (Goodison Park)	0–3
1963	v Manchester United (Goodison Park)	4–0
1966	v Liverpool (Goodison Park)	0–1
1970	v Chelsea (Stamford Bridge)	2–1
1984	v Liverpool (Wembley)	1–0
1985	v Manchester United (Wembley)	2–0
1986	v Liverpool (Wembley)	1–1
1987	v Coventry City (Wembley)	1–0
1995	v Blackburn Rovers (Wembley)	1–0

Everton won the Charity Shield for four successive years in the 1980s, though they shared it with Liverpool in 1986.

* In 1932, Dixie Dean scored four of Everton's goals in their 5–3 win at Newcastle United.

CHEDGZOY, SAM. Ellesmere Port-born Sam Chedgzoy played his early football with Burnell's Ironworks alongside Joe Mercer's father. Although he made his Everton debut in a 1–0 defeat at Newcastle United on Boxing Day 1910, it was another four seasons before he established himself as a first-team regular. In that 1914–15 season, he helped Everton to win the league championship. In 1920, he won the first of his eight international caps when he played for England against Wales at Highbury. In the match against Tottenham Hotspur at White Hart Lane on 12 April 1924, Sam Chedgzoy caused the game's rules to be re-written. A new rule had been adopted under which a goal could be scored direct from a corner. Chedgzoy took the corner-kick by dribbling the ball along the by-line and hammered it into the net in Everton's 5–2 win. Twelve months later, the game's hierarchy introduced a new rule which stated that the taker of the corner-kick could play the ball only after a second player had touched it. Chedgzoy went on to score 36 goals in 300 league and Cup games for Everton before retiring at the end of the 1925–26 season and emigrating to Canada.

CLEAN SHEET. This is the colloquial expression used to describe a goalkeeper's performance when he does not concede a goal. Gordon

West in 1969–70 kept 21 clean sheets from 42 league appearances, helping the Blues to win the league championship. Goalkeeping legend Ted Sagar kept 18 clean sheets from 41 league appearances when Everton won the first division title in 1938–39. Interestingly, in the game that Sagar was forced to miss, Everton travelled to Molineux and lost 7–0 to Wolverhampton Wanderers, with replacement keeper Morton having a nightmare game.

CLEMENTS, DAVE. The winner of 48 Northern Ireland caps, Dave Clements began his career as a winger with Wolverhampton Wanderers. Failing to make the grade at Molineux, he joined Coventry City in 1964 for £1,000. It was whilst at Highfield Road that he was converted into a half-back and went on to play in 277 league games for the Sky Blues before leaving to join Sheffield Wednesday in the summer of 1971 for a fee of £100,000. At Hillsborough, he played mainly at full-back but after appearing in 78 league games, he moved to Everton for £60,000 in September 1973. He made his debut in a 1–1 draw at his first club Wolverhampton Wanderers, and over the next three seasons went on to prove himself one of the club's most intelligent players. On 18 March 1975, he was playing for Everton at Middlesbrough when he learned he had been appointed manager of Northern Ireland. He played the last of his 98 games for the club in a 3–3 home draw against Ipswich Town in December 1975. He later joined New York Cosmos but his decision to play in America cost him his job as his country's manager.

CLENNELL, JOE. A little demon on the ball, Joe Clennell played in junior football in his native north-east with the likes of Silksworth United and Seaham Harbour before entering the Football League with Blackpool. Then he played for Blackburn Rovers before joining Everton in January 1914. Making his debut at home to Aston Villa at the end of the month, he scored Everton's goal in a 4–1 defeat. On the opening day of the 1914–15 season he scored a hat-trick as the Blues beat Tottenham Hotspur 3–1 at White Hart Lane. He went on to score 17 goals in 41 league and Cup appearances as the club won the first division championship and reached the semi-finals of the FA Cup. In wartime football, Clennell played in 124 games for the Blues, scoring 128 goals including four in a match on five occasions. When the Football League resumed in 1919, he continued to find the net with great regularity and scored a hat-trick in a 4–1 home win over Bradford City. Injury curtailed his Everton career and in October 1921 he joined Cardiff City. He later played for Stoke before moving to Bristol Rovers and Rochdale. He didn't stay anywhere for long at this time, but his growing affinity with Wales showed through when he became player-manager of first Ebbw Vale, then Barry Town and Bangor before going to Great Harwood. He later managed Distillery in the Irish League and coached Accrington Stanley.

CLINTON, THOMAS. Full-back Thomas Clinton, who went on to win international honours with the Republic of Ireland, was signed in the most unusual of circumstances. He had been recommended to Everton by a local scout and so Theo Kelly travelled to Ireland to discuss terms. As he chatted with Clinton on the platform of Dundalk Station, the young defender's train began to pull out and he actually put pen to paper while hanging out of a lowered carriage window. He made his first-team debut for Everton in a 2–1 home win over Burnley in February 1949 and over the next five seasons went on to appear in 80 league and Cup games. During the FA Cup semi-final against Bolton Wanderers in 1953, Clinton missed a penalty in the last minute of the first-half with the Wanderers leading 4–0. Though the Blues scored three second-half goals, it just wasn't enough to complete what would have been an epic recovery. In 1955, Clinton joined Blackburn Rovers but after just a handful of appearances he moved to Tranmere Rovers where he ended his league career.

COCA-COLA CUP. See Football League Cup.

COCK, JACK. A naturally gifted centre-forward, Jack Cock always gave the impression that he played the game for laughs. A typically robust target man, he could score with both feet and his head, and indeed during his career he netted over 200 league goals. Described as a sophisticated socialite who loved to dress in expensive clothes, Cock actually came from a poor family of ten and a humble background in Cornwall. During the First World War he was reported 'missing presumed dead' but he won a Military Medal and, after the hostilities had ended, he joined Chelsea. He won the first of two England caps against Ireland at Belfast in 1919 and scored England's goal in a 1–1 draw. He scored again in his second game as England came back from 4–2 down to beat Scotland 5–4 at Sheffield in April 1920. He left Stamford Bridge in January 1923 to join Everton, and made a goalscoring debut as the Toffees beat Stoke 4–0. Later that season, he scored a hat-trick in a 5–3 home win over Middlesbrough. He had netted 31 goals in 72 games when in March 1925 he joined Plymouth Argyle. He later helped Millwall to the third division (South) championship in 1927–28 and in 1944 became their manager, helping them to the Football League (South) Cup final.

COGGINS, BILLY. When goalkeeper Billy Coggins arrived at Goodison Park from Bristol City in April 1930, the only other custodian on the Everton books was a very young Ted Sagar. Coggins made his debut for the Blues in a 4–2 home defeat by Grimsby Town, a result which condemned the club to relegation from the first division. In 1930–31, Coggins was an ever-present as Everton raced away with the second division championship. The following season, Coggins played in only one game as Sagar launched his outstanding career and the Blues went on to win the league championship. Unhappy with reserve-team football, he played the last of his 56 games in February 1934, before leaving to play for Queens Park Rangers and later Bath City.

COLLINS, BOBBY. Bobby Collins joined Everton straight from Scottish junior football but was desperately homesick and returned north of the border to sign for Glasgow Celtic. He made his international debut for Scotland against Wales in 1951 and made 22 full international appearances during his stay at Parkhead. In September 1958, he rejoined the Blues for a fee of £39,000 and made a goalscoring debut in a 3–1 win over Manchester City at Maine Road only hours after putting pen to paper. He stood at 5ft 4ins and weighed only 10st 3lbs, but he continued to find the net with regularity during his four seasons at Goodison. In 1959–60 he was the club's only ever-present and leading scorer with 14 goals. The following season he scored 16 league goals including hat-tricks against Newcastle United (home 5–0) and Cardiff City (home 5–1). In March 1962, after scoring 48 goals in 147 league and Cup games, he surprisingly left Goodison Park to join Leeds United for £30,000. Many saw it as a backward step, especially as the Elland Road club seemed destined to drop into the third division. However, over the next three seasons, the Yorkshire side won promotion and narrowly missed the league and Cup double. Despite breaking a thigh bone in an Inter-Cities Fairs Cup match in Turin, Collins fought his way back to play in 149 league games before joining Bury on a free transfer in 1967. After a spell at Morton, he coached in both Australia and South Africa. In October 1972, he became player-coach of Oldham Athletic, later taking charge at Hull City, Huddersfield Town and Barnsley.

COLOURS. In October 1881, when Everton were playing in blue-and-white striped shirts, they were joined by a number of players from other clubs who brought their own jerseys with them. In order to save costs it was decided to obtain uniformity by dyeing all jerseys black and to wear a two-inch wide sash over them. The shirts led to the club's first nickname, 'The Black Watch'. The following year they changed to salmon pink and later to ruby shirts with blue trimmings and shorts. It wasn't until 1901 that they made the switch to royal blue shirts, white shorts and blue socks. The club's change colours are amber shirts with black stripes, black shorts and amber socks.

CONNOLLY, JOHN. A talented winger, always willing to take on his full-back, John Connolly began his career with St Johnstone before joining Everton for £75,000 in March 1972. He missed just one game of the 1972–73 season after playing in a couple of matches towards the end of the previous campaign. Twice he had to fight his way back from a broken leg but such was the Scottish winger's courage. In 1973 he made his full international debut against Switzerland but this was also the year when Billy Bingham replaced Harry Catterick as manager and Connolly never really hit it off with the Irishman. After scoring 16 goals in 116 games, he was placed on the transfer list at his own request and in September 1976 he moved to Birmingham City for a fee of £90,000, teaming up with former colleagues Gary Jones and Howard Kendall. He didn't stay long at St Andrews and was soon on his way to Newcastle United. He appeared in 49 league games for the Magpies before returning north of the border to end his career with Hibernian.

CONSECUTIVE HOME GAMES. Everton played an extraordinary sequence of eight home league and Cup games in succession in 70 days, 3 January 1903–14 March 1903. They won six – Middlesbrough (3–0), Wolverhampton Wanderers (2–1), Sheffield United (1–0), and Bury (3–0) in the league; Portsmouth (5–0) and Manchester United (3–1) in the FA Cup. They lost 1–0 to Aston Villa and 3–0 to Sunderland in the last of the eight league matches.

CONSECUTIVE SCORING – LONGEST SEQUENCE. Dixie Dean holds the club record for consecutive scoring when he was on target in 12 consecutive league games. The sequence started when he scored four goals in Everton's 6–4 home win over Oldham Athletic on 6 December 1930 and ended with two goals in a 5–2 win over Barnsley, also at Goodison Park, on 18 February 1931. Dean scored a hat-trick at Charlton Athletic on 7 February, and totalled 23 goals in the 12 games.

COOK, BILLY. An Irish international right-back, Billy Cook joined Everton from Celtic for £3,000 in December 1932 and made his debut in a 2–1 home defeat by West Bromwich Albion on the last day of the year. At the end of his first season at Goodison Park, he joined the élite band of players to have won both a Scottish Cup winners' medal and an FA Cup winners' medal as Everton beat Manchester City 3–0 at Wembley. He won his Scottish Cup winners' medal in 1931 when Celtic beat Motherwell 4–2 after a 2–2 draw. By the start of the 1938–39 season, Cook had played in over 200 games without scoring a goal, a statistic he put right during this campaign with six league and Cup strikes. Though he played in 93 wartime games for the club, he joined Wrexham in October 1945, moving to Rhyl as player-manager 12 months later. Following a spell as Sunderland's coach he was appointed coach to the Peruvian FA in Lima. His travels took him on to Norway before he returned to England to take charge at Wigan Athletic.

COTTEE, TONY. An England Youth international, Tony Cottee made a sensational first-team debut for West Ham United, aged 17, scoring after 26 minutes in the match against Tottenham Hotspur on New Year's Day 1983. In 1985–86, he was capped for the England Under-21 team, won the PFA Young Player of the Year award and the Fiat Uno Young Player of the Year. Forming good striking partnerships with Paul Goddard and later Frank McAvennie, Cottee was rewarded with a full international debut against Sweden in September 1986. Returning to Upton Park, he scored two hat-tricks in the space of three days and ended the season as the club's top scorer with 22 goals. He left Upton Park in the summer of 1988 to join Everton for a club record fee of £2.3 million. He quickly settled into the Goodison club's side and marked his debut with a stunning hat-trick in a 4–0 win against Newcastle United on the opening day of the 1988–89 season, including scoring his first goal after just 34 seconds. Although there were occasions when his team-mates didn't play to his strengths, he ended each of his first three seasons at the club as Everton's leading marksman. Cottee regularly found himself at odds with his manager and in August 1989 he was fined £5,000 after refusing to turn out in a reserve-team fixture. He went on to score 99 goals in 241 league and Cup games for Everton before rejoining the Hammers in September 1994. He continued to score on a regular basis for West Ham but in October 1996 he was sold to Selengor. Now playing in the Premier League for Leicester City, Cottee scored 145 goals in his two spells with West Ham, the most prolific Upton Park striker since Geoff Hurst.

COULTER, JACKIE. Born and raised in Belfast, Jackie Coulter played his early football with Cliftonville before joining Belfast Celtic. It was from here that he signed for Everton in 1934 for a fee of £3,000, making his debut in a 1–1 home draw against Portsmouth on 21 April 1934. The following season he soon established himself in the Everton side and scored 17 goals in 29 league and Cup games including a hat-trick in a 6–4 FA Cup fourth-round replay win over Sunderland. After breaking his leg whilst playing for Northern Ireland against Wales at Wrexham in 1935, he was never the same player again and in late 1937 he was allowed to join Grimsby Town. One of the game's most unorthodox wingers, Coulter later played for Swansea and non-league Chelmsford before leaving the game.

CRELLEY, JACK. Though he was born in Liverpool, Jack Crelley was one of a number of north-west footballers recruited by Southern League club, Millwall Athletic. He returned to Merseyside in 1899 and made his debut for Everton in a goalless draw against Blackburn Rovers, though it was 1902–3 before he became a regular in the Blues first team. Forming a good full-back partnership with Walter Balmer, he played left-back in Everton's successful 1906 FA Cup final side but missed out a year later when Robert Balmer was selected alongside his elder brother for the 2–1 defeat by Sheffield Wednesday. A strong-tackling and sturdy defender, Crelley appeared in 127 league and Cup games for Everton before leaving to join Exeter City in 1907.

CRESSWELL, WARNEY. One of the game's classiest defenders, Warney Cresswell began his career with South Shields and when he left to join Sunderland in 1922 for £5,500, it was a British record. He joined Everton in February 1927 and made a disastrous debut in a 6–2 defeat at Leicester City. Nevertheless, he retained his place in the side and over the next ten seasons was a regular member of an Everton side that won two league championships, the FA Cup and the second division championship. His only goal for the club came in a 4–2 home defeat by Manchester United towards the end of the 1928–29 season. In 1929, he played for England against Northern Ireland, so winning his seventh full cap. After having appeared in 306 league and Cup games for the Goodison club, he left in the summer of 1936 to become manager-coach of Port Vale. Twelve months later he was appointed manager of Northampton Town, a position he held for two years before taking charge at non-league Dartford.

CRICKETERS. Jack Sharp and Harry Makepeace were double internationals playing cricket and football for England. Signed from Aston Villa, Jack Sharp scored 81 goals in 342 games for Everton, appeared in the FA Cup finals of 1906 and 1907 and was capped twice by England. For Lancashire he scored 22,015 runs at an average of 31.38 and hit 38 centuries. A fast-medium bowler, he took 434 wickets at 27.23 runs each and held 223 catches. He appeared in three Tests and in 1909 scored 105 against Australia. Harry Makepeace played in 336 games for Everton and won four international caps at half-back for England. For Lancashire, he scored 25,207 runs at 36.37 and in four Test matches, all of them abroad, he scored 279 runs including 117 in the Melbourne Test of 1921.

CRITCHLEY, TED. Discovered playing in junior football in his native Stockport, Ted Critchley signed for Stockport County and after the flying winger became a first-team regular in the Edgeley Park club's side, a number of top-flight clubs showed an interest in signing him. Therefore it was not surprising when, in December 1926, he joined Everton for a fee of £3,000. Within three days of his transfer, he made his debut for the Blues in front of a Christmas Day crowd of 37,500, creating four goals for Dixie Dean in a 5–4 win over Sunderland. He was a key member of Everton's league championship-winning side and was instrumental in helping Dixie Dean achieve his unsurpassable record of 60 league goals in one season. Two years later, the Blues suffered the trauma of relegation but they bounced back immediately, winning the second division title with Critchley scoring 15 goals. Twelve months later, the first division championship trophy was again on display in the Goodison trophy cabinet. Critchley scored 42 goals in 229 league and Cup games for the Blues before leaving to join Preston North End in 1934. He ended his league career with Port Vale.

CROSSLEY, CHARLIE. Though he had only one full season in the Everton side, the Walsall-born inside-forward was the club's top scorer. Signed from Sunderland in the summer of 1920, Charlie Crossley played his first game for the club in the 3–3 draw at Bradford on the opening day of the 1920–21 season. Forming an exciting left-wing partnership with George Harrison, Crossley went on to score 18 league and Cup goals, including a spell of 16 in 22 games. Yet in 1921–22, his form was less consistent and he found himself in and out of the Everton first team. At the end of the season, he was transferred to West Ham United. He played in 14 games as the club won promotion to the top flight, but he was unable to find a place in the Hammers side that played Bolton Wanderers in the first Wembley Cup final.

CROWD TROUBLE. In December 1895, torrential rain brought the game with Small Heath to a halt and with the referee in two minds about whether to postpone it or not, the players stormed off the field of play, annoyed at his indecision. When he finally did decide to continue with the game, some of the players were already having a bath, so he called it off. Many of the crowd demanded their money back and were reinforced by an army of street loafers. Although they were offered free tickets for the replay, a riot ensued, windows and woodwork were smashed and there was a move to set fire to the stands before contingents of police arrived to drive the mob away with batons.

CUNLIFFE, JIMMY. Jimmy Cunliffe arrived at Goodison Park from Adlington FC in 1930 and after three years in the club's Central League side, he scored on his first-team debut in a 2–1 defeat at Aston Villa. In 1933–34, he deputised for the injured Dixie Dean and when the legendary centre-forward returned to the side, Cunliffe moved to inside-right. The following season, he scored a last-minute equaliser in the fourth-round FA Cup game against Sunderland at Roker Park and then produced a magnificent display in the replay which Everton won 6–4. In 1935–36, Cunliffe was the club's leading goalscorer with 23 goals in 37 league games, including scoring four goals in the victories over Stoke City (home 5–1) and West Bromwich Albion (home 5–3). It was this form that led to him winning his only cap for England against Belgium at Brussels in 1936. He continued to score with great regularity and netted a hat-trick in a 7–0 win over Derby County on Christmas Day 1936, ending his career with 76 goals in 187 league and Cup games.

CUPS. In its history, the club has won 15 major trophies – nine league championships, five FA Cups and one European Cup-Winners' Cup.

D

DARRACOTT, TERRY. One of Everton's most popular players, Terry Darracott made his debut for the club in a 2–0 home win over Arsenal in April 1968 while still an apprentice. Though he never really hit the heights as a player, only establishing himself in 1973–74, he played in 176 first-team games over ten seasons with the Goodison club. In 1979, Everton manager Gordon Lee offered him the post of youth-team coach but Darracott preferred to continue playing and joined Wrexham, for whom he played in 27 league and Cup games. He became player-coach at Prescot and in May 1985, he returned to Goodison as reserve-team coach. Six months later, he left to work alongside Mike Lyons at Grimsby Town but in the summer of 1986, he rejoined Everton as managerial assistant to Colin Harvey. Following the return of Howard Kendall in November 1990, Darracott was sacked, but three months later linked up with another Everton old-boy, Peter Reid, at Manchester City.

DAVIES, DAI. Born in the South Wales mining village of Ammanford, Dai Davies began his career in local football before joining Swansea Town. After only nine league appearances for the Swans, he signed for Everton in December 1970 for £25,000. After spending virtually four seasons in the shadow of Gordon West and his understudy David Lawson, Davies went back to Vetch Field on loan. He returned to Goodison and went on to appear in 94 league and Cup games before leaving to join Wrexham. Whilst with Everton he gained the first of 52 Welsh caps when he played in Wales' 2–1 win over Hungary in Budapest. In his first season at the Racecourse Ground, Wrexham

Dixie Dean

suffered the lowest number of defeats in their history as they won the third division championship. In 1978–79, Davies helped establish the club's best-ever league defensive record of only 42 goals conceded. The Robins won the Welsh Cup and qualified for Europe. At the end of the 1980–81 season, Davies returned to play for Swansea before becoming player-coach at Tranmere Rovers in the summer of 1983. He retired from the game a year later but when Bangor City qualified for Europe in 1985, they called on Davies' experience, against Fredrikstad and Atletico Madrid, as did Wrexham in the 1985–86 Welsh Cup competition.

DEAN, DIXIE. Arguably the greatest goalscorer that the game has ever known, Dixie Dean carved a very special niche for himself in Merseyside sporting folklore. Born on the other side of the Mersey, he once scored 18 goals in a day, six goals each in three games. In the morning he played in a Birkenhead Schoolboys trial, in the afternoon he turned out for Laird Street School and in the evening he played for Moreton Bible Class. He made his league debut for Tranmere Rovers during the 1923–24 season, but it was during the following campaign that he gave notice that he was about to become a major force in the game when he played in 27 games and scored 27 goals, at the age of 17.

Everton were one of the first clubs to spot his talents and Tom McIntosh, the club secretary, was sent over the water to sign the young player. Dean was delighted when he arrived home to be told by his mother that an Everton official had been wanting to talk to him. He was so excited that he ran the three miles to the Woodside Hotel to meet McIntosh and signed for the Blues there and then. Five days later, on 21 March 1925, he made his debut in a 3–1 defeat against Arsenal at Highbury. A week later, he made his home debut and scored a goal in Everton's 2–0 win over Aston Villa. In his first full season with the club, he scored 32 goals in 38 games including hat-tricks against Burnley (away 3–1), Leeds United (home 4–2), Newcastle United (away 3–3) and Newcastle United (home 3–0). The pinnacle of his career was reached in 1927–28 when he scored 60 goals in 39 league games, including all five in a 5–2 home win over Manchester United and four in a 5–3 win at Burnley, as well as five hat-tricks. A measure of the centre-forward's indomitable spirit was his recovery from a bad road accident in the summer of 1926. He came very close to death in a motor-cycle crash which left him unconscious for 36 hours with a broken jawbone and a fractured skull. His remarkable constitution and iron will pulled him through and within 15 weeks of the accident he was back in the club's Central League side. A fortnight later, in October 1926, he was back and scoring in the Blues' first team. In that memorable 1927–28 season, Dean started the last game of the season against Arsenal needing a hat-trick to pass George Camsell's record of 59 goals set the previous year. He achieved the feat in spite of the Gunners scoring three times, and not only established a new goalscoring record but Everton also clinched the league title. In 1938 he severed his ties with the Goodison club when he joined Notts County. When they totted up the statistics at the end of his illustrious Everton career, he had worn the blue shirt on 431 occasions and scored 377 goals. He had been capped 16 times by his country and won every honour the game could bestow upon him. After playing in just nine games for Notts County, he moved on to the Irish club Sligo, but the Second World War interrupted and he retired from the game to run the Dublin Packet pub in Chester. Sadly, in 1976 his right leg was amputated after a long illness. Four years later at Goodison Park, just minutes before the final whistle of the Merseyside derby, he collapsed and died. It was perhaps fitting that the club's most gifted son should have died while watching the club that he had made famous.

DEBUTS. Fred Pickering and Tony Cottee are the only players to have scored hat-tricks on their first-team playing debuts for the club.

Pickering scored three in the Blues' 6–1 win over Nottingham Forest on 14 March 1964, whilst Cottee hit three against Newcastle United on 27 August 1988, Everton winning 4–0. Paul Bracewell holds the rare distinction of making his Everton debut at Wembley; after signing from Sunderland for £250,000 at the end of the 1983–84 season, he played in the Charity Shield showpiece against Liverpool three months later.

DEFEATS – FEWEST. During the 1969–70 season, Everton went through the 42-match programme with only five defeats, winning the first division championship. They also suffered five defeats in 1889–90 but that was from a 22-match programme.

DEFEATS – MOST. Everton's total of 22 defeats during the 1950–51 season is the worst in the club's history. Not surprisingly, they finished bottom of the first division and were relegated.

DEFEATS – WORST. Everton's record defeat was when Tottenham Hotspur beat them 10–4 at White Hart Lane on 11 October 1958. The club's worst home defeat came on Boxing Day 1933 when Newcastle United visited Goodison Park and won 7–3.

DEFENSIVE RECORDS. Everton's best defensive record over a 42-match Football League season was established in 1986–87 and helped the club win the first division championship. They conceded just 31 goals in that campaign and were beaten in only eight matches. The club conceded just 29 goals in 1890–91 when they first won the league title, but that was from only 22 games. Everton's worst defensive record was in 1929–30 when they conceded 92 goals, finished bottom of the first division and were relegated for the first time in the club's history.

DISMISSALS. Neville Southall and Paul Rideout hold the unenviable record of being the first Everton players to be dismissed in a Premier League game when they got their marching orders in the match against Queens Park Rangers at Loftus Road on 28 December 1992. For the record, Everton lost 4–2. The Everton keeper was sent off a second time later that season as the Blues went down 3–1 at Sheffield Wednesday. Although sendings-off are an all too common feature of the modern game, no one should imagine that football has ever been immune from them. As Everton challenged for the league championship in 1904–5, England international Tom Booth was sent off with his namesake Frank, the Manchester City forward, during a vital end-of-season clash, which City won 2–0, in an infamous off-the-ball incident. In the mid-1960s, Sandy Brown was sent off after just a few minutes of a bad-tempered encounter with Leeds United. In fact, the referee later had to take both teams off the field for a cooling-down period. Everton's Brian Kidd became only the third player in the history of the FA Cup to be sent off in a semi-final when he was dismissed against West Ham United in 1980. Craig Short will certainly remember his European debut. He was sent off in Rotterdam in the final minutes of a Cup-Winners' Cup tie against Feyenoord for elbowing former Dutch international Ronald Koeman.

DOBSON, MARTIN. Martin Dobson started his career as a centre-forward with Bolton but in 1967 the Wanderers gave him a free transfer. He considered giving up the game but his father persuaded Burnley manager Harry Potts to give him a trial at Turf Moor. Dobson joined the Clarets as a front runner but was eventually switched to midfield where he won international recognition, being called up for England Under-23s against Bulgaria at Plymouth. In 1972–73, he captained Burnley to the second division championship and the following season led them to sixth place in the first division and to the semi-finals of the FA Cup. Four days after the semi-final, he won the first of five full international caps in a goalless draw against Portugal. In August 1974, Dobson moved to Goodison Park for £300,000, a new British transfer record. He made his debut for the Blues in a 2–1 home win over Arsenal and, in five years at Everton, he was always a first-team regular. He figured in two UEFA Cup campaigns and in 1977 played in the FA Cup semi-final defeat by Liverpool and the three-game, marathon League Cup final, which ended in defeat by Aston Villa. In the 1978–79 League Cup campaign, he scored a hat-trick when Everton achieved their best scoreline, 8–0, against Wimbledon in a second-round tie. Bob Latchford hit the other five. It was perhaps a surprise when Dobson returned to Turf Moor in the summer of 1979 for £100,000 after scoring 40 goals in 230 league and Cup games for the Blues. After failing to halt the Clarets' slide to the third division, he once again captained the club and in 1982–83 led them to the third division championship. He moved to Bury in 1984, later becoming player-manager and then manager of Bristol Rovers. He is now Youth Development Officer for his first club, Bolton Wanderers.

DODDS, EPHRAIM. Known to everyone as 'Jock', Ephraim Dodds played his early football in Lanarkshire and Durham before joining the staff at Huddersfield Town. Two years later he signed for Sheffield United on a free transfer and in four seasons with the Bramall Lane club topped the scoring lists. In 1939, he joined Blackpool for a fee of £10,000 and in 15 games scored 13 goals before the Second World War intervened. He appeared in 164 wartime games for the Bloomfield Road club, scoring 228 goals. Though Dodds was never to win a full Scotland cap, he did represent his country eight times in wartime internationals. Immediately after the war, Everton were struggling to find a centre-forward and in November 1946 they signed Dodds. He made his debut against Grimsby Town, scoring one of the goals in a 3–3 draw. He ended that season as the club's top scorer with 17 goals in 21 games. He repeated the achievement in 1947–48, scoring 13 goals in 27 games, including hat-tricks against Wolverhampton Wanderers (away 4–2) and Huddersfield Town (away 3–1). His third and final hat-trick for the club was on 25 September 1948 when Everton beat Preston North End 4–1 at Goodison Park. He had scored 37 goals in 58 league and Cup games when, in October 1948, he was transferred to Lincoln City. When he retired from the game, he had scored 198 league goals in 305 games for his four clubs.

DONNACHIE, JOE. One of the greatest far-post crossers of the ball, Joe Donnachie began his career with Newcastle United before joining Everton in 1906. He made his debut in a goalless draw at Notts County and went on to appear in 42 games for the club before leaving to play for Oldham Athletic. Able to play on either wing, he won three Scottish caps during his stay at Boundary Park, his last in 1915. After the First World War, he went to play for Glasgow Rangers before returning to Everton for a second spell in the summer of 1919. He later played for Blackpool, ending his league career with Chester.

DONOVAN, DON. Donal Donovan, his first name was shortened to Don by his Everton team-mates, was discovered purely by chance on the club's pre-season tour of Eire in the summer of 1949. Manager Cliff Britton and a number of Everton's directors were taking a stroll in Cork when they came across a local amateur cup-tie. Playing for Maymount Rovers at inside-right, Donovan did enough to be asked to join Everton's junior school. After working his way through the ranks, he made his first-team debut in a 3–3 home draw against Sheffield Wednesday in August 1951. By now, he had been converted to wing-half and after helping the club win promotion to the first division in 1953–54, won the first of five full caps for the Republic of Ireland when he played against Norway. He scored only two goals in his 187 games for the club; one was a spectacular 35-yard strike against Manchester United at Old Trafford. Everton won that game 5–2, easing their relegation worries and ending United's run of 26 league games without defeat. Donovan played his last game for the club against Manchester City in April 1958, by which time he had replaced Peter Farrell as the Blues captain.

DOWNS, DICKIE. Known as the 'Indian Rubber Man', full-back Dicky Downs, who some claim invented the sliding tackle, appeared in two FA Cup finals for Barnsley in 1910 and 1912 before joining Everton for £3,000 in March 1920. He made his debut in a 1–0 defeat against Manchester United at Old Trafford but his form in the 12 games that remained of the 1920–21 season led to him making an international appearance for England against Ireland. He was rarely out of the side during his three years with the club, but in 1923, after playing in 97 games, he left to join Brighton. Twelve months later, injury forced his retirement and he went abroad, coaching in Germany and Holland.

DRAWS. The Blues played their greatest number of drawn league matches in a single season in 1925–26, 1971–72 and 1974–75, when 18 of their matches ended all-square; and their fewest in 1890–91 when only one of their 22 matches was drawn. The club's highest scoring draw is 5–5, a scoreline in two games – Derby County (away 1898–99) and Sheffield Wednesday (away 1904–5). In this last game, played on 12 November 1904, Everton went in at half-time 5–0 up, but early in the second half they lost their goalkeeper, Billy Scott, through injury and Wednesday came back well to share the points.

DUBAI GOLD CUP. In December 1987, Everton had an eight-hour journey for a challenge match with Glasgow Rangers in Dubai. The Blues were playing well, cruising along with a two-goal lead, until a misdirected back-pass found one of the Rangers players and gave the Scottish club the encouragement to stage a fight-back. Suddenly the Ibrox club were level and forced a penalty shoot-out. It turned out to be a remarkable competition because the first 15 penalties were all converted. That made it 8–7 for Rangers when Ian Snodin took the 16th kick. He hit it quite well but the keeper guessed the right way to dive and made a very good save.

DUGDALE, GORDON. Having played for Bootle and Lancashire Schoolboys, Gordon Dugdale joined Everton on his demob from the Royal Navy in 1947. He made his debut at left-back in a 1–1 home draw against Wolverhampton Wanderers on 4 October 1947 and, over the next three seasons, developed into a superb defender. Strong in the tackle and a good distributor of the ball, he looked certain to be involved in England's 1950 World Cup team when he was compelled to give the game up. During his service in the Far East as a pilot in the Fleet Air Arm, he had developed a heart complaint and it suddenly recurred after he had made just 63 league and Cup appearances for the Blues. Though he never scored for Everton, he did score a remarkable own goal in a game at Middlesbrough when he tried to chip the ball back to Ted Sagar, only for it to sail over his head and into the roof of the net. In 1952, he became a director of South Liverpool FC and later stood as Conservative candidate for the Low Hill ward.

DUNLOP, ALBERT. One of Everton's most reliable goalkeepers, Albert Dunlop made his debut in a 5–2 win at Manchester United in October 1956, seven years after joining the club! He went on to appear in 59 consecutive league games before injury cost him his place. Over the next six seasons, he was the club's first-choice keeper and in 1960–61 when the club finished fourth in the first division after six seasons of mid-table mediocrity, he was an ever-present. Dunlop, who had a safe pair of hands and instilled confidence into his defenders, played the last of his 231 games for the club in a 4–1 home win over Fulham on the final day of the 1962–63 season. He had a spell with Wrexham before leaving league football. Unfortunately, his personal life became something of a disaster as he was put on probation for two years after being found guilty on charges of deception.

DUNN, JIMMY. Inside-forward Jimmy Dunn joined Everton from Hibernian in the summer of 1928 and made his debut for the Goodison club at Bolton on the opening day of the 1928–29 season when Dixie Dean netted all the Blues' goals in a 3–2 win. In 1930–31, he helped Everton win the second division championship, scoring 14 goals in 28 games. In 1931–32, he scored a hat-trick on the opening day of the season as the Blues won 3–2 at home to Birmingham, ending the campaign with ten goals in 22 games as the club won the first division championship. The following season, he scored one of Everton's goals in the 3–0 FA Cup final win over Manchester City. A Scottish international, winning six caps for his country, he played the last of his 154 first-team games, in which he scored 49 goals, on the final day of the 1934–35 season. He was transferred to Exeter City. He had three footballing sons. The most famous was Jimmy Dunn junior, who was an England Schoolboy international and who won an FA Cup winners' medal with Wolverhampton Wanderers in 1949.

E

EARLY GROUNDS. Everton began life as St Domingo's, playing their early football in the south-east corner of Stanley Park. There were no changing-rooms. Players collected the goalposts from the Park Lodge in Mill Lane and fixed them into sockets in the ground. During the 1879–80 season, the club changed its name to Everton and in its first match under its new name, beat St Peters 6–0. When Everton played Bootle, as many as 2,000 spectators would turn up. It was the problem of so many spectators that caused the club to abandon Stanley Park and move to Priory Road. A small stand and a dressing-room were constructed and the club continued to play matches against local sides, such as Haydock and the Liverpool Ramblers, as well as teams from further afield, such as Burslem and Hartford St Johns from Cheshire. In the 1883–84 season, the club won its first trophy, beating Earlestown 1–0 in the final of the Liverpool Cup. Yet despite this success, Mr Cruitt, the owner of the Priory Road field, had grown tired of the noise and crowds that were flocking to the ground and Everton were told in no uncertain terms to find another venue for their matches. John Orrell, a friend of John Houlding, a prominent citizen who became Lord Mayor of Liverpool, had a patch of land in the Anfield Road and said the club could rent the ground providing they kept it in good condition and made a donation each year to the Stanley Hospital in his name. The club played their first match at Anfield Road on 27 September 1884, beating Earlestown 5–0, and, encouraged by winning the Liverpool Cup for two years in succession, entered the FA Cup. One of the founder members of the Football League, Everton played their first match against Accrington at Anfield, winning 2–1.

After winning the league title in 1890–91, John Orrell increased the rent for the ground. Houlding came up with a counter plan – the club would form a limited company and approach Orrell with an offer to purchase the ground. Unknown to the public, Houlding had bought land adjoining Anfield and the purchase of the ground included the purchase of his land. On 25 January 1892, Houlding's proposal was thrown out and Orrell reacted by giving the club notice to quit, which they did.

EASTOE, PETER. A former England Youth international, Tamworth-born forward Peter Eastoe began his career with Wolverhampton Wanderers. The Molineux club were well off for strikers with Derek Dougan, John Richards and Alan Sunderland on their books, and so after just four league appearances, Eastoe was allowed to join Swindon Town for £80,000. He proved himself to be a prolific goalscorer at the County Ground, netting 43 goals in 91 matches before being transferred to Queens Park Rangers for a fee of £100,000. He didn't seem to settle at Loftus Road and in 1979 he joined Everton in an exchange deal involving Mick Walsh. He made his debut as a substitute for Dave Thomas in a 1–0 defeat at West Bromwich Albion on 7 April 1979. He was hampered by injuries the following season, but in 1980–81 he was an ever-present and the club's leading scorer with 19 goals. He went on to score 33 goals in 115 league and Cup games before moving to West Bromwich Albion in the summer of 1982 in a straight exchange for Andy King.

EBBRELL, JOHN. A former England Schoolboy and Youth international, John Ebbrell made his debut as a central midfield player in Everton's 4–0 home win over Newcastle United on the opening day of the 1988–89 season. He went on to win 14 England Under-21 caps and also represented the England B side. Ebbrell was the club's midfield anchorman, a player similar in style to ex-Blues star Peter Reid. Operating in front of the back four, the strong-tackling Ebbrell would break up the opposition's attacks and, using his main asset of accuracy, send telling passes to his own forwards. He had scored 17 goals in 253 league and Cup games before he joined Sheffield United for £1 million in March 1997.

EGLINGTON, TOMMY. One of the club's greatest-ever servants, Tommy Eglington missed very few games for the Blues in the 11 years after the Second World War, making 428 league and Cup appearances and scoring 82 goals. He joined Everton along with Peter Farrell from

Tommy Eglington

Shamrock Rovers for a joint fee of £10,000, the deal proving to be one of the best strokes of business that the club has ever pulled off. Eglington made his league debut for the Blues in a 3–2 home win over Arsenal in September 1946. His speed and trickery earned him 24 full caps for the Republic of Ireland and another six for Northern Ireland. He appeared alongside Peter Farrell in the historic game at Goodison Park in 1949 when the Republic of Ireland defeated England 2–0. This was the first time England had been defeated on home soil by a non-British team. Eglington guaranteed himself a place in the pages of Everton's history when, on 27 September 1952, he almost single-handedly demolished Doncaster Rovers at Goodison Park by scoring five goals in a 7–1 win. A player with intricate close control and stunning shooting power, Tommy Eglington left Everton for Tranmere Rovers in 1957, playing nearly 200 games for the Prenton Park club before returning to his native Dublin, where he now runs a butcher's shop.

EUROPEAN CUP. Everton's first excursion into the European Cup in 1963–64 was brief. They drew Italian champions Inter Milan and a Goodison Park crowd of over 63,000 paid £31,450 to see the game, a record figure for a club match in England apart from the FA Cup final. The game itself was goalless with the Blues unable to break down Inter's defensive blanket. A week later, Everton were out of the

European Cup, losing 1–0 in the San Siro Stadium to a Jair goal. If Dennis Stevens had been on target towards the end of the game in Everton's only chance of the match, then anything could have happened. The club's second time in the European Cup competition was 1970–71. On 16 September 1970, Alan Ball netted a hat-trick in a 6–2 win over Icelandic champions Keflavik and the Blues extended the aggregate to 9–2 after the away leg. In the second round, Everton met Borussia Moenchengladbach; both ties ended 1–1 and the Blues went through on penalty kicks. On 3 March 1971, Greek champions Panathinaikos visited Goodison for the first leg of the quarter-final tie. In a bruising encounter, David Johnson scored for Everton in a 1–1 draw but it was a game the Blues should have won; they hit the woodwork four times. Three weeks later on a noisy night in Athens, both teams failed to score and so the Greeks went through on the away goals rule.

EUROPEAN CUP-WINNERS' CUP. After winning the FA Cup in 1966, the Blues' entry into the European Cup-Winners' Cup the following season was short-lived. The first round brought a narrow 2–1 aggregate victory over Aalborg, the Danish Cup winners, after the first leg in Denmark had been goalless. The Blues' next opponents were Real Zaragoza who defeated Everton 2–0 in the beautiful Spanish cathedral town. Although a Sandy Brown goal gave the Goodison club a 1–0 win in the home leg, it wasn't enough to take them into the third round. In 1984–85, the club drew part-timers University College Dublin in the first round but returned from Ireland with a goalless draw. In the second leg, only a Graeme Sharp goal separated the teams and Everton could consider themselves fortunate to be in the second round. The Blues travelled to Czechoslovakia to play Internacional Bratislava and came away with a one-goal lead, courtesy of Paul Bracewell. The second leg ended 3–0 in Everton's favour, giving the club a comfortable win on aggregate. In the quarter-final, an Andy Gray hat-trick gave them a 3–0 win over Fortuna Sittard of Holland. In the second leg, Everton attacked the Dutch side just as keenly as they had at Goodison and won 2–0 with goals from Reid and Sharp. The club's opponents in the semi-final were Bayern Munich. In front of a 70,000 crowd packed into the Munich Olympic Stadium, the Blues defended stubbornly to come away with a goalless draw. At Goodison, it was a night to remember as the Blues came from a goal behind to win 3–1 with goals from Gray, Sharp and Steven. The Blues' opponents in the final were Rapid Vienna. Some 50,000 spectators gathered in Rotterdam and though Everton were the better side, they couldn't turn their superiority into goals. Eventually Andy Gray broke the deadlock, slamming home a Graeme Sharp cross. Trevor Steven hit a second, driving home a Sheedy corner, but with ten minutes to go, the Austrian side pulled a goal back. Within a minute, Everton had hit back, Sheedy breaking free of the Rapid defence to make it 3–1. The club last participated in the European Cup-Winners' Cup in 1995–96. They beat Reykjavik of Iceland 6–3 on aggregate in the first round, although at half-time in the second leg they were 1–0 down (3–3 on aggregate). In the second round, Dutch side Feyenoord provided the opposition and the Blues went out 1–0 on aggregate after a goalless first leg at Goodison.

EVER-PRESENTS. There have been 57 Everton players who have been ever present throughout a league season. The greatest number of ever-present seasons by an Everton player is six by Neville Southall.

F

FA CUP. Everton entered the FA Cup for the first time in 1886–87 and were drawn against Glasgow Rangers, but on the eve of the game they found they couldn't hope to beat the Scottish side unless they fielded players who were ineligible for the competition. They decided to play their strongest team – lost 1–0 – and then scratched from the competition. Everton's biggest victory in the FA Cup came in season 1889–90 when they defeated Derby County 11–2. The club reached the final for the first time in 1893 but lost 1–0 to Wolverhampton Wanderers. Five years later, the Blues appeared in the final again only to lose 3–2 in a classic match against Aston Villa. The Blues first won the FA Cup in 1906 when a Sandy Young goal was enough to beat Newcastle United 1–0. They reached the final again the following year but lost 2–1 to Sheffield Wednesday. The club had to wait until 1933 before their next appearance in the final, beating Manchester City 3–0 with goals from Dean, Dunn and Stein. Everton returned to Wembley in 1966 and in one of the most memorable finals of modern times beat Sheffield Wednesday 3–2 after being two goals down. Two years later, the Blues were back at Wembley again but lost 1–0 to West Bromwich Albion in extra-time. The club won the Cup a fourth time in 1984, beating Watford 2–0 with goals from Gray and Sharp. In 1985, Manchester United ended the Blues' hopes of an astonishing treble (league championship, European Cup-Winners' Cup and FA Cup) by winning 1–0 in the final. The following season, Everton reached the final for the third consecutive year only to be beaten 3–1 by their Merseyside rivals. The two teams met in the final again in 1989 with Liverpool winning 3–2 after extra-time; Stuart McCall scored both Everton goals. The club

51

reached the final for the 12th time in 1995 and beat Manchester United, the Cup holders, 1–0; Paul Rideout scored the all-important goal.

FA CUP FINALS. Everton have appeared in 12 FA Cup finals, winning the trophy on five occasions. In 1966, they reached the final without conceding a goal – the last team to do so.

1893	Wolverhampton Wanderers (Fallowfield)	0–1
1897	Aston Villa (Crystal Palace)	2–3
1906	Newcastle United (Crystal Palace)	1–0
1907	Sheffield Wednesday (Crystal Palace)	1–2
1933	Manchester City (Wembley)	3–0
1966	Sheffield Wednesday (Wembley)	3–2
1968	West Bromwich Albion (Wembley)	0–1
1984	Watford (Wembley)	2–0
1985	Manchester United (Wembley)	0–1
1986	Liverpool (Wembley)	1–3
1989	Liverpool (Wembley)	2–3
1995	Manchester United (Wembley)	1–0

FA CUP SEMI-FINALS. Everton hold the record for the most appearances in FA Cup semi-finals with 23 up to the end of the 1997–98 season.

Peter Farrell

FARRELL, PETER. Peter Farrell's career coincided with that of Tommy Eglington. They both arrived at Everton from Shamrock Rovers in the summer of 1946, and Farrell joined Tranmere Rovers as player-manager in October 1957, four months after Eglington had joined the Prenton Park club. The Dublin-born wing-half was one of only a handful of players to appear in full internationals both for Northern Ireland and the Republic of Ireland. He represented Northern Ireland seven times when they could select players born in the Republic for the Home International championship. He won the first two of his 28 caps for the Republic of Ireland after the war when he was still playing for Shamrock Rovers, and his first with Everton against Spain in 1947. In 1949 he helped to make history when he scored one of the goals for the Republic of Ireland against England at Goodison Park. The Republic became the first non-British team to defeat England at home. An inspiration to all around him, very popular on the field, Farrell was also something of a hero off it, mixing freely with the club's supporters in a down-to-earth manner. He captained the side for a number of years and in 11 seasons at Goodison Park, appeared in 453 league and Cup games. His spell at Tranmere was not the happiest of experiences and after posts at Wrexham and Holyhead, he returned to Ireland to continue in management.

Duncan Ferguson

FERGUSON, DUNCAN. A target man who is a handful for defenders, Duncan Ferguson began his career with Carse Thistle before making his name at Dundee United. He made his full international debut for Scotland against the United States in 1992 but it was his club form that attracted bids of over £3 million from Bayern Munich, Chelsea and Leeds United, all of which were turned down. However in 1993, Ferguson joined Glasgow Rangers for a then British transfer record fee of £4 million. A serious knee injury hampered his progress with the Scottish champions and in two seasons at Ibrox 'Big Dunc' made only 14 starts. When he signed for Everton after a loan period at Goodison Park, he set another British transfer record by becoming the first player to be transferred twice between British clubs for a fee of £4 million or more. He is the only British professional footballer to go to prison for assaulting a fellow pro during a match. On 11 October 1995, he was sentenced to three months in Barlinnie Prison for head-butting Raith Rovers full-back John McStay during a match at Ibrox. The Scottish FA weighed in with a 12-match ban. A hernia operation reduced the player's role in the 1995 FA Cup final to that of substitute, and niggling injuries dogged him from the start of the 1995–96 campaign. Holding the ball up well and lethal at set-pieces, he was the club's leading scorer for the next two seasons, though disciplinary problems continue to plague one of the game's most promising careers.

FERN, TOM. Goalkeeper Tom Fern joined Everton from Lincoln City in 1913, filling the gap left by the departure of Billy Scott to Leeds City. He made his debut in a 1–1 home draw against Sheffield Wednesday and kept clean sheets in his next four games for the club. In 1914–15, he missed just two games as the Blues won the league championship. That same season, Everton reached the FA Cup semi-final but Fern was injured and missed the 2–0 defeat by Chelsea at Villa Park. Fern was also injured when Everton played Crystal Palace in the 1921–22 FA Cup competition but, despite a damaged hand, he played in the infamous 6–0 thrashing by the London club. That was the game during which Palace's goalkeeper Jack Alderson was eating oranges at the other end! Always in the thick of the action, Fern would have added to his 231 first-team appearances had it not been for the First World War, but in 1924 he left Goodison to sign for Port Vale, appearing in 90 games for the Valiants.

FEWEST DEFEATS. During Everton's first division championship winning season of 1969–70, the club went through the 42-match programme losing only five games. The first of these came at Derby

County on 6 September when, despite a goal from Howard Kendall, they lost 2–1. The club's next defeat didn't come until 8 November when they lost 2–0 at West Bromwich Albion after winning 15 and drawing two of the previous 17 matches. Two of the other defeats were also away from home – Leeds United (1–2) and Southampton (1–2) whilst the club's only defeat at Goodison Park came at the hands of Liverpool who won 3–0.

FIELDING, WALLY. Before he joined the army, Wally Fielding was on Charlton Athletic's books as an amateur. He went to the Middle East where his form as a scheming inside-forward was good enough to get him into army representative sides. When he left the army in 1945, Charlton believed that they held the right to his continued services. But Theo Kelly, Everton's manager, pipped them for his signature and he made his league debut in a 2–0 home defeat by Brentford in the opening game of the 1946–47 season. He made the Number 10 shirt his own over the next 12 years, appearing in 410 league and Cup games for the Blues. One of his trademarks was his perfectly weighted passes inside the full-back to Tommy Eglington. He was more than capable of looking after himself in the face of the most ferocious tackles. Though never a prolific marksman, he carried a powerful and accurate shot and netted 54 goals in his Goodison career. Dubbed as 'Merseyside's answer to Len Shackleton', he made only one appearance in the white shirt of England, that being in the Bolton Disaster Fund game against Scotland at Manchester in 1946, a game that did not count as an official full cap. Fielding was a chirpy character and a most positive influence on the Everton youngsters who used to copy his mannerism of clutching his rolled-down shirt-sleeves as he ran. He was nearing 40 when he left Everton for Southport in 1959 but still bubbling with enthusiasm.

FINES. In 1966, Everton were fined £2,000 for not fielding a full side for the match against Leicester City (which they lost 3–0) a few days before the FA Cup final. They won at Wembley through two goals by reserve forward Mike Trebilcock. In August 1989, Tony Cottee was fined £5,000 by the club after refusing to play in a reserve-team fixture at Coventry City. Everton fined Neville Southall a week's wages for staging a sit-down protest at half-time in their opening match of the 1990–91 season. The club were fined £125,000 for poaching the Norwich City manager Mike Walker to replace Howard Kendall in 1994.

FIRST DIVISION. Everton were members of the first division from the 1888–89 season until the end of the 1929–30 season when they suffered relegation for the first time in their history. They played their first match against Accrington at Anfield, winning 2–1 with both goals scored by Fleming. The following season, the Blues scored in every league match. The only other first division team ever to achieve this feat was Bolton Wanderers. In 1890–91, Everton overcame the challenge of Preston North End to become the second club to win the league title. The club won their last four Division One matches of 1893–94 and the first eight of the 1894–95 season for a winning sequence of 12 games. Everton's second league championship success came in 1914–15 when only three points separated the top ten clubs. The club's 46 points was the lowest total since the first division was expanded to 20 clubs. Everton won the first division title for a third time in 1927–28 as Dixie Dean scored 60 goals in 39 league appearances. An alarming slump the following season meant Everton finished fifth from bottom of the first division, followed by relegation for the first time in the club's history in 1929–30. Promoted immediately, the Blues won the league title for a fourth time in 1931–32. They did so having lost 12 games during the season – the most defeats by a team winning the Football League title. Everton won a fifth title in 1938–39 as they re-fashioned their side around the skills of young players such as Tommy Lawton and Joe Mercer. Relegated at the end of the 1950–51 season, it was 1953–54 before promotion was gained. During the latter half of the 1950s, the club hovered in the lower reaches of the first division and it wasn't until 1960–61 when Johnny Carey took them to fifth place that the Blues showed any improvement. Yet John Moores decided that Carey wasn't the man for the job and brought in Harry Catterick. In 1962–63, the club swept to the title for a sixth time, unbeaten at home and setting a new club record points total. The 1969–70 campaign capped anything that had gone on before as a seventh title was secured with a new record points tally for Everton of 66. Everton became the first Football League club to reach 3,000 matches in the first division when they visited Brighton and Hove Albion on 7 October 1980. The Blues won the title for an eighth time in 1984–85. This season they set another club record when they won ten consecutive matches. Gary Lineker became the club's most expensive purchase during the summer of 1985 but the Blues could only finish runners-up to Liverpool. In 1986–87, despite injuries to a number of key players, Everton won their ninth title, a second success in three years. Over the next few seasons, the club's league form, especially at home was inconsistent and relegation to the new first division seemed likely. However, thankfully it wasn't to be and the Blues kicked off the 1992–93 season in the newly formed Premier League.

FIRST LEAGUE MATCH. In Everton's first match in the newly formed Football League, they entertained Accrington on 8 September 1888. The match kicked off some 20 minutes late, Accrington having lost their way to the ground. The visitors won the toss, but surprisingly opted to kick into the sun. All the early attacking was from Everton, though Accrington almost snatched the lead against the run of play when Holden headed against Smalley's crossbar. Both Lewis and Dobson went close for Everton before Chadwick missed the easiest chance of the match two minutes from half-time. Everton went ahead after 60 minutes when Farmer's left-wing cross was met perfectly by Fleming who headed into the bottom corner of Horne's goal. Within a minute, Everton's Lewis kicked a shot off the line with Smalley beaten as Accrington pressed for an equaliser. Fifteen minutes from full-time, the visitors goalkeeper, Horne, was carried from the field with a fractured rib after colliding with Chadwick. McLennon took over but within a couple of minutes had conceded a goal, Everton's second, scored again by Fleming. Holden did reduce the arrears for Accrington after heading against the crossbar and in the final minute, only a brave save from Smalley prevented Accrington from equalising. Everton's team was: R. Smalley, N. Ross, A. Dick, G. Dobson, J. Holt, R. Jones, G. Farmer, A. Chadwick, W. Lewis, D. Waugh and G. Fleming.

FIRST MATCH. Everton FC played their first match against St Peters on 20 December 1879. Auspiciously, Everton won 6–0. The local newspaper reported the score only – no teams or scorers – so the names of the players in Everton's first-ever team will probably always remain unknown.

FLEETWOOD, TOM. A versatile half-back, Tom Fleetwood joined the club from Rochdale in 1911 and made his debut in a goalless draw at home to Bradford City in March of that year. Equally at home in any of the half-back positions, he also turned out at centre-forward in emergencies. When the First World War broke out, he had appeared in 147 first-team games, but went on to play some of his best football during the hostilities. He appeared in 121 wartime games for the Toffees and such was his form that he made two appearances for England in Victory internationals against Scotland. He had won a league championship medal with the Goodison Park club in 1914–15 but by the time he was awarded a benefit match against Sheffield United in 1921–22, the Blues were playing badly and so the attendance was much less than might have been hoped for. He went on to play in 285 league and Cup games for the club before leaving in the summer of 1923 to play for Oldham Athletic.

FLOODLIGHTS. The Goodison Park floodlights were switched on for a friendly against second division neighbours Liverpool on 9 October 1957 to mark the 75th anniversary of the Liverpool County Football Association. They were changed in 1971, the pylons being replaced by ultra-powerful lights on the roofs of the stands, the Bullens Road Stand being reroofed in the process.

FOOTBALLER OF THE YEAR. The Football Writers' Association Footballer of the Year award has been won by Everton players on two occasions:

1984–85	Neville Southall
1985–86	Gary Lineker

The Professional Footballers' Association award for Player of the Year has also gone to two Everton players:

1984–85	Peter Reid
1985–86	Gary Lineker

FOOTBALL LEAGUE CUP. The club first took part in the competition in 1960, the initial game taking place at Goodison where the Blues beat Accrington Stanley 3–1. Everton have reached the League Cup final on two occasions, the first being in 1976–77 when they met Aston Villa in a dire affair which ended goalless. The teams met again at Hillsborough a few days later. It was a match Roger Kenyon would want to forget as he put through his own goal but then, with just one minute to go, he crossed for Bob Latchford to slam home the equaliser. Extra-time brought no further goals and so the teams met a month later at Old Trafford. After 90 minutes the score stood at 2–2 and the game went into extra-time again. With just 90 seconds remaining, Brian Little scored for Villa to win the Cup for the Midlands side. In 1983–84, the Blues met Liverpool at Wembley. It was the game all Merseyside had dreamed of for almost a century. Goalless after 90 minutes, extra-time was necessary, but again neither side was able to break down what were arguably the best two defences in

Europe. The replay at Maine Road four days later was settled by a Graeme Souness goal that skidded past Neville Southall. The club's best scoreline in the League Cup came in the second round of 1978–79 when Wimbledon were beaten 8–0 with Bob Latchford (5) and Martin Dobson (3) the scorers. Neville Southall holds the record for number of appearances in the competition for the club with a total of 63 between 1982 and 1997 whilst Bob Latchford heads the goalscoring chart with 19.

FREEMAN, BERTIE. After playing for Aston Villa and Arsenal, the Birmingham-born forward joined Everton from the Gunners in 1908 as a replacement for Sandy Young. He played in the last four games of the 1907–8 season, and created a new first division record the following season, when he scored 38 goals in just 37 games. He scored two against his former club Woolwich Arsenal in the opening game of the season and went on to net hat-tricks against Sheffield United (away 5–1), Sunderland (home 4–0), Sheffield United (home 5–1) and Chelsea (home 3–2). He topped the club's scoring charts again in 1909–10 with 22 goals in the league and a further four in FA Cup games, including hat-tricks against Sheffield Wednesday (away 3–1) and Bolton Wanderers (home 3–1). That season he played in the North v South England trial at Fulham and later won two full caps against Wales and Scotland as well as scoring four goals for the Football League against the Irish League. After three seasons with the Blues, in which he scored 67 goals in 94 league and Cup games, he was surprisingly allowed to leave Goodison and join Burnley. In 1914, he scored the only goal of the FA Cup final against Liverpool to take the Cup to Turf Moor.

FULL MEMBERS' CUP. In their first game in this competition, Everton beat Newcastle United 5–2 with Scottish international centre-forward Graeme Sharp grabbing a hat-trick. In the second round, the Blues entertained Charlton Athletic. At full-time, the score was 2–2 but in the ensuing penalty shoot-out, the visitors from the second division triumphed by 6–4.

G

GABRIEL, JIMMY. Jimmy Gabriel became one of the most expensive teenagers in British football when he joined the Goodison club from Dundee for £30,000 in March 1960. Within 72 hours of signing, he made his debut in a 2–2 draw at West Ham United, but in only his third game for the club he came up against West Bromwich Albion's England forward Derek Kevan. It was an afternoon the young Gabriel would never forget as the West Brom 'Bomber' scored five goals in a 6–2 win for his team. But the Scotsman reacted positively, volunteering for extra training to hone his fitness as he acclimatised to the more rigorous demands of the Football League. Gabriel went on to build a fine career in which he played 301 first-team games for the Blues. A powerhouse of a right-half, particularly effective in defence, he was the perfect foil for the adventurous wanderings of Brian Harris from left-half. An ever-present in 1961–62 he played a major part in the club's league championship success the following season and was a member of the Blues' victorious FA Cup side of 1966. On 18 March 1967, he was sent to Blackpool with the reserves whilst the newly signed Howard Kendall was making his league debut against Southampton. It was the beginning of the end of his Goodison career. Gabriel moved to The Dell where he appeared in 191 league games in five years of yeoman service. After a spell with Bournemouth, he moved to North America where he played for Seattle Sounders. He returned to Everton in the summer of 1990 to help manager Colin Harvey look after the first team, later taking over as caretaker boss before Kendall's second coming. Since then, he has remained part of the Goodison club's coaching set-up, but it's as an accomplished top-flight performer when

Jimmy Gabriel

the Blues had their backs to the wall that Everton fans will forever remember Jimmy Gabriel.

GALT, JIMMY. Jimmy Galt began his career with Glasgow Rangers, winning three Scottish League championship medals and a Scottish Cup runners-up medal in his time at Ibrox. He also won two Scottish caps and played four times in the Glasgow v Sheffield fixture. He signed for Everton in the 1914 close season and played his first game for the club in the 3–1 win at Tottenham Hotspur on the opening day of the 1914–15 season. He was made club captain and that season led the Blues to the league championship and to the semi-finals of the FA Cup. Unfortunately, his Goodison career was ruined by the outbreak of the First World War and he played in just one wartime game before officially leaving the club to play for Third Lanark in October 1920.

GEARY, FRED. Nottingham-born Fred Geary played his early football with two of his home-town clubs, Notts County and Notts Rangers, but it was from Grimsby Town that Everton signed him in 1889. He scored twice on his debut in a 3–2 home win over Blackburn Rovers and ended the season as the club's top goalscorer with 21 goals in 18 league games, including a hat-trick in an 8–0 win over Stoke. He topped the club's scoring charts again in 1890–91, hitting 20 goals in 22 games, including 11 in the opening six fixtures. It was this kind of form that led to him winning international recognition and on his debut he scored a hat-trick in England's 9–1 win over Ireland in Belfast. He also represented the Football League against the Scottish League, picking up one of the first gold medals struck to commemorate the fixture. After suffering a series of injuries in 1891–92, he was back to his best form the following campaign, again topping the club's goalscoring charts with 19 in 24 games, including another hat-trick in a 6–1 win at Derby County. Though he continued to score on a regular basis, his appearances were less frequent and in 1894, after netting 86 goals in 98 appearances, he moved to Anfield where he ended his playing days.

GEE, CHARLIE. Stockport-born centre-half Charlie Gee began his league career with his home-town club Stockport County whom he joined from Reddish Gren Wesleyans. He made 27 first-team appearances for the Edgeley Park club before joining Everton in the summer of 1930. He spent the first six months at Goodison Park in the reserves before making his league debut in a 3–2 home win over Bury, when he scored one of the goals. By the end of the season he was a first-team regular and won a second division championship medal. The following season he won the first of three international caps when he played against Wales at Anfield and ended the campaign with a league championship medal as the Toffees swept to successive titles. In 1932–33, he suffered a cartilage injury and though he reclaimed his place the following season he was never quite the same player. He had made 211 appearances up to the outbreak of the Second World War, playing his last game for the Blues at Fulham in the fourth round of the 1939–40 League War Cup.

GELDARD, ALBERT. Albert Geldard was the youngest footballer ever to play in a Football League match. He was 15 years 156 days old when he turned out for Bradford Park Avenue at Millwall in September 1929. He joined Everton as an 18-year-old in November 1932 and scored on his debut in a 2–0 win at Middlesbrough. One of the game's fastest wingers, he laid on the pass which enabled Jimmy Dunn to score Everton's third goal in the 1933 FA Cup final win over Manchester City. Also in 1933, he won the first of four full England caps whilst with Everton when he played against Italy. Geldard was not slow to cut inside and shoot and in the third-round FA Cup tie against Grimsby Town in January 1935 he netted a hat-trick in a 6–3 home win. He went on to score 37 goals in 179 league and Cup games for the Blues

John Gidman

before joining Bolton Wanderers for £4,500 in 1938. He appeared in 39 games for the Wanderers before ending his career in 1946–47. Unusually, he was a member of the Magic Circle.

GIDMAN, JOHN. Although he was born in Liverpool, John Gidman began his league career with Aston Villa. He was an important member of their FA Youth Cup-winning team of 1972 and enjoyed eight successful seasons with the Midlands club, winning one England cap and a League Cup winners' tankard in 1977. After scoring nine goals in 242 games, he moved back to Merseyside to join Everton who paid a club record fee of £650,000 in October 1979. Gidman made his Everton debut in a goalless home draw against Manchester United. Although he spent less than two years at the club, he made 78 league and Cup appearances. He moved to Manchester United in a swap deal that took Mickey Thomas to Goodison Park and immediately slotted into the Old Trafford club's defence. After that, Gidman had mixed fortunes, he almost lost an eye in a fireworks accident, and suffered from injuries. He fought his way back to win an FA Cup winners' medal against Everton in 1985 but at the end of the following season he was given a free transfer. He joined Manchester City, later signing for Stoke City, where he was forced to retire because of injury in 1990.

GILLICK, TORRY. A well-built winger, Torry Gillick joined Everton from Glasgow Rangers in December 1935 for a fee of £8,000 and made his debut in a goalless draw at home to Leeds United. Able to play on either flank, he won five full caps for Scotland during his time at Goodison, the first against Austria in 1937. Gillick was an entertainer, sometimes brilliant, at other times infuriating. He was an exhilarating sight when he was in full flight, and helped to maintain the tradition of top-class Scottish players at Goodison. He had scored 44 goals in 133 games when the Second World War broke out and so, sadly, the Everton fans never saw his best years. When the game resumed after the hostilities, Gillick had left the club, having returned to Rangers in November 1945.

GOALS. The most goals Everton have ever scored in one game was their 11–2 victory against Derby County in an FA Cup first-round game at Anfield Road on 18 January 1890. Alec Brady, Fred Geary and Alf Milward all scored hat-tricks with Foyle and Kirkwood scoring a goal apiece. In the Football League, Manchester City were beaten 9–1 on 3 September 1906 in a first division game and Plymouth Argyle by the same scoreline in a second division game on 27 December 1930. The Blues have also beaten Stoke (2 November 1889) and Southampton (20 November 1971) by an 8–0 scoreline.

GOALS – CAREER BEST. The highest goalscorer in the club's history is Dixie Dean who, between seasons 1924–25 and 1937–38, netted 377 goals for the club. These comprised 349 in the league and 28 in the FA Cup.

GOALS – INDIVIDUAL. The man who scored the highest number of goals for Everton in a league match was Jack Southworth. He hit six in a 7–1 win over West Bromwich Albion on 30 December 1893. A week earlier, he had scored four goals in an 8–1 win over Sheffield Wednesday and between 9 December 1893 and 13 January 1894 he registered 16 goals. A number of players have scored five goals in a game for Everton. Dixie Dean and Tommy Lawton each achieved the feat on three occasions. Dean's five goals came in the matches against Manchester United (home 5–2 on 8 October 1927), Sheffield

Wednesday (home 9–3 on 17 October 1931) and Chelsea (home 7–2 on 14 November 1931). Lawton's five goals all came in wartime matches – Tranmere Rovers (home 9–2 on 6 November 1943), Crewe Alexandra (away 6–2 on 15 January 1944) and Crewe Alexandra again (away 5–1 on 25 November 1944). Tommy Eglington scored five goals in a 7–1 home win over Doncaster Rovers on 27 September 1952 whilst the last Everton player to achieve the feat was Bob Latchford in an 8–0 League Cup win over Wimbledon on 29 August 1978. In the club's pre-league days, a player by the name of Fraser scored eight of Everton's goals in a 14–0 Liverpool Cup win over New Ferry.

GOALS – SEASON. The club's highest league goalscorer in any one season remains Dixie Dean who scored a remarkable 60 league goals as Everton won the first division championship in 1927–28. He also scored three goals in the FA Cup to take his season's tally to 63. In the league, he scored all five goals against Manchester United (home 5–2) and four against Burnley (away 5–3) and hat-tricks against Portsmouth (away 3–1), Leicester City (home 7–1), Aston Villa (away 3–2), Liverpool (away 3–3) and Arsenal (home 3–3).

GOALKEEPERS. In 1904–5, Everton signed Welsh international goalkeeper Dr Leigh Richmond Roose. The club had hopes of winning the league and Cup double that year – first division runners-up and FA Cup semi-finalists – and Roose's sometimes outrageous antics between the posts made a lasting impression on those who saw him play. Succeeding Roose was Billy Scott. He was Everton's keeper in their 1906 and 1907 FA Cup finals and he won three league championship runners-up medals with the club. Everton legend Ted Sagar was one of the finest goalkeepers of all time. He spent an astonishing 24 years with the club between 1929 and 1953 – the longest spell any player has had professionally with one club. He played in a record number of league games for the Blues which was surpassed by Neville Southall, another of the club's outstanding goalkeepers. Southall's brilliant reflexes allow him to make astonishing point-blank saves. The automatic choice for Wales, having made his debut in 1982, he holds the record for the most international appearances for his country.

GOALSCORING EXPLOITS. The first division goalscoring record – 42 set by Blackburn Rovers' Ted Harper in 1925–26 – seemed a remote target when Dixie Dean notched his first goal of the 1927–28 season after 75 minutes of Everton's 4–0 home win over Sheffield Wednesday. Dean started to attract speculation soon afterwards when he found the net in each of the club's first nine matches, which included all five in the 5–2 home win over Manchester United on 8 October 1927. The first time he failed to score was the following week in the local derby at Goodison which ended 1–1. The first landmark that Dean passed came on 2 January 1928 when his two goals in a 4–2 defeat at Blackburn took him past Bobby Parker's club record of 36 goals set in 1914–15. More significantly, his hat-trick in a memorable 3–3 draw with Liverpool at Anfield took his tally to 43, beating Harper's record. With nine games left, Dean needed 17 goals to break George Camsell's total of 59 for Middlesbrough the previous season. The bookmakers offered 10,000 to 1 against Dean reaching his 60 goal target. He missed one of the last nine matches but scored in the other eight. When the final game came against Arsenal at home, Dean needed a hat-trick – he duly obliged and when he scored his third goal, the Goodison crowd of 48,715 exploded!

GOLDEN VISION. A television play, entitled *The Golden Vision*, centred around the Everton club in the 1960s and was inspired by Alex Young, signed from Hearts in November 1960. Young made 271 league and Cup appearances for the Goodison Park club and scored 87 goals.

GOODISON PARK. Goodison Park was formally opened on 24 August 1892 by Lord Kinnaird, president of the Football Association. After a dinner at the Adelphi Hotel, Kinnaird and a host of city dignitaries travelled by carriage to the ground, where a short ceremony was followed by an evening of athletic events, culminating in a magnificent fireworks display. The first game played at Goodison Park was on 2 September 1892 when the Blues beat Bolton Wanderers 4–2. In their first league fixture of 1892–93, Everton could only manage a 2–2 draw against Nottingham Forest. The ground was honoured in 1894 when Notts County beat Bolton in the FA Cup final in front of a disappointing crowd of 37,000. The Goodison of today really began to take shape after the turn of the century, starting in 1907 with the building of the Park End double-decker stand at a cost of £13,000. In 1909, the large Main Stand on Goodison Road was built. It cost £28,000, housed all the offices and player facilities and survived for 43 years. Around this time another £12,000 was spent on concreting over the terracing and replacing the cinder running track. One of the best-equipped grounds in England, Goodison was chosen to host the 1910 FA Cup final replay between Barnsley and Newcastle United and, in 1913, became the first league ground to be visited by a ruling monarch when King George V and Queen Mary came to meet local schoolchildren at the ground. The next major development was in 1926

Goodison Park

when at a cost of £30,000 another double-decker, similar to the Main Stand, was built on the Bullens Road site opposite. Another royal visit occurred in 1938 when King George VI and Queen Elizabeth, the present Queen Mother, inspected the Gwladys Street Stand, just completed for £50,000. During the Second World War, Goodison suffered quite badly because it lies near the docks, and the club received £5,000 for repair work from the War Damage Commission. Shortly after the work was completed, Everton enjoyed their highest attendance, 78,299 for the visit of Liverpool in a first division match on 18 September 1948. The Goodison floodlights were originally mounted on four extremely tall pylons and were switched on for a friendly against Liverpool on 9 October 1957. A year later, the club spent £16,000 on installing 20 miles of electric wiring underneath the pitch. The system melted ice and frost effectively but the drains could not handle the extra load, so in 1960 the pitch was dug up again and new drainage pipes laid. In 1966, Goodison staged five games in the World Cup, more than any other ground apart from Wembley. In 1971, the 1909 double-decker Main Stand in Goodison Road was demolished to make way for a new three-tiered Main Stand. The new stand cost £1 million and, at nearly twice the size of its predecessor, was the largest in Britain at that time.

Because the Goodison Road Stand is so tall, the floodlight pylons were taken down and lamps put on gantries along the roof. In August 1994, the new £2.4 million Park End Stand with seating for 6,000 opened. Because of its crucial place in the history of football grounds and the atmosphere which prevails here on special occasions, Goodison Park is still one of the best grounds in the country.

GOODLASS, RONNIE. After a number of impressive displays for England Schoolboys, Ronnie Goodlass began to attract the attention of several top clubs, but having been born just down the road from Goodison Park, he was more than happy to sign for Everton. An old-fashioned type of winger, always willing to take on defenders and get to the by-line, he made his debut on 23 December 1975 in a 1–1 home draw against Manchester United. He was an important member of the Everton side which reached the semi-finals of the FA Cup and the League Cup final in 1976–77 but following the arrival of Dave Thomas from Queens Park Rangers in August 1977, his opportunities were limited. He joined Dutch club Breda for £75,000 and later played for Den Haag before returning to England to play for Fulham. After just 22 league appearances for the Cottagers, he joined Scunthorpe United before trying his luck in Hong Kong. Becoming homesick he returned to Merseyside to play with Tranmere Rovers in 1983, later joining non-league Barrow.

GRANT, JACKIE. A versatile player, Jackie Grant played in seven different positions in his Everton career. Signed in December 1942, he made his debut against Liverpool in a League North wartime match and went on to appear in 92 games for the club during the hostilities. A highly competitive player, he made his league debut in a 2–0 home defeat by Wolverhampton Wanderers in October 1946. It was to be another four seasons before he won a regular place in the Everton line-up, but he was the star of the club's 3–2 FA Cup fourth-round replay win over Wolverhampton Wanderers in January 1948. He made two goals for Wally Fielding and then scored the winner himself. He played in all the club's games during their relegation season of 1950–51 but after that his appearances were limited and he spent most of the rest of his time at Goodison Park captaining the reserve side to Central League successes. After playing in 133 league and Cup games, he joined Rochdale in the summer of 1956 before ending his career with Southport.

GRAY, ANDY. One of the bravest strikers of his generation, Andy Gray began his career with Dundee United, scoring 44 goals in 76 games for

Andy Gray

the Tannadice club. He signed for Aston Villa for £110,000 in September 1975. In 1976–77, when Villa finished fourth in the first division and beat Everton in the final of the League Cup, Gray was the club's top scorer with 29 goals in 48 appearances. He was voted PFA Player of the Year and Young Player of the Year. After four years at Villa Park he moved to Wolverhampton Wanderers for a British record fee of £1.5 million. Four years later he moved again, this time to Everton for £250,000. He made his debut in a 1–0 home win over Nottingham Forest and ended the season scoring the Blues' second goal in the 1984 FA Cup final win over Watford. He also scored the first goal in the 1985 European Cup-Winners' Cup triumph over Rapid Vienna and at the end of the season he was dramatically recalled into the Scotland side, eventually ending with 20 full caps to his name. He had scored 22 goals in 68 league and Cup games when he rejoined Villa for £150,000. After a loan spell at Notts County, he signed for West Bromwich Albion but retired shortly after his arrival at the Hawthorns. In the summer of 1991, he returned to Villa Park for a third time as assistant manager to Ron Atkinson. He resigned in 1992 to pursue a career in television with Sky.

GREENHALGH, NORMAN. After starting his career with his home-town club Bolton Wanderers, Greenhalgh joined New Brighton in 1935, playing 77 league games for the third division (North) club before signing for Everton midway through the 1937–38 season. He had played his early football at right-half before settling at right-back, but when he returned to action after an appendix operation at New Brighton, he played a number of games up front. However, at Goodison he reverted to his more familiar role of right-back, forming a good full-back partnership with the ferocious-tackling Willie Cook. He was an ever-present when the Toffees won the league championship in 1938–39, a season when he represented the Football League. After appearing in 254 wartime games, he returned to league action in 1946–47 but two seasons later played the last of his 115 league and Cup games in a 6–0 defeat at Chelsea. Given a free transfer he joined Bangor City, where he saw out his career.

GRENYER, ALAN. Signed from his home-town club, South Shields, wing-half Alan Grenyer made his Everton debut in a 2–1 home win over Nottingham Forest in April 1911 but over the next couple of years made only four first-team appearances. With Lancashire and England cricketer Harry Makepeace holding down the left-half position, it was the championship-winning season of 1914–15 before he became fully established. His goal in the 2–1 win at Bradford Park Avenue took the Blues to the top of the table for the first time that season and with only two games to play they hung on to win their second league title. During the First World War, Grenyer played in 119 games for Everton, his form winning him a place in the England side for a Victory international against Wales. He played the last of his 148 senior games for the club, in which he scored nine goals, against Chelsea in February 1923 before returning home to sign for North Shields.

GRIFFITHS, TOM. Tom Griffiths was a tall, no-nonsense centre-half who began his career with Wrexham, playing in 53 first-team games for the Racecourse Ground club. He joined Everton in 1927 and made his debut in a 6–2 defeat at Leicester City. He had to wait a further 20 months before playing in his second game for the club, missing the entire 1927–28 season when the Blues won the league championship. Yet despite not appearing in the Goodison Park club's first team,

Griffiths had succeeded the immortal Fred Keenor as the regular Welsh centre-half; in 1927 he was selected against England for the first of eight caps he won whilst with Everton. A regular member of the Everton side in seasons 1928–29 and 1929–30, he played in all the 23 games of the 1930–31 campaign before losing his place through injury to Charlie Gee. Later, he had spells with Bolton Wanderers and Middlesbrough before ending his career with Aston Villa. Despite some heroic performances, he couldn't prevent their relegation.

GUEST PLAYERS. The guest system was used by all clubs during both world wars. Although on occasions it was abused almost beyond belief (some sides that opposed Everton had ten or eleven guests), it normally worked sensibly and effectively and to the benefit of players, clubs and supporters. During the First World War, a number of Everton players drifted to Lancashire clubs. During the Second World War, Everton's Cliff Britton and Joe Mercer joined with Wolverhampton Wanderers' Stan Cullis and made Aldershot one of the strongest of wartime teams with the England half-back line on call.

H

HAMILTON, BRYAN. A terrier-like midfield player, Bryan Hamilton began his Football League career with Ipswich Town after moving there from Linfield. He went on to score 56 goals in 199 games for the Portman Road club before signing for Everton for £40,000 in 1975. He made his debut for the Blues in a 5–2 defeat at Leeds United and over the next two seasons played in 54 league and Cup games. He played for Everton in the League Cup final of 1977, although he will always be remembered on Merseyside for scoring 'the goal that never was'. In the FA Cup semi-final against Liverpool, the game stood at 2–2 when, with just seconds remaining, Hamilton hammered the ball past Ray Clemence's despairing dive, apparently clinching Everton's place at Wembley. For no reason whatsoever, referee Clive Thomas ruled out the Irishman's effort and Liverpool went on to win the replay 3–0. Hamilton later played for Millwall and Swindon Town before joining Tranmere Rovers as player-manager. Sacked in 1985, he led Wigan Athletic to Wembley success in the Freight Rover Trophy final before taking charge at Leicester City. He returned to Springfield Park in 1988 but lost his job in 1993 as the Latics struggled to get away from the foot of the first division. Capped 50 times for Northern Ireland, he became the national manager until replaced by Lawrie McMenemy in 1998.

HARDMAN, HAROLD. One of the game's smallest players, Manchester-born winger Harold Hardman joined Everton from Blackpool in the summer of 1903 and made his debut in the opening game of the 1903–4 season, scoring the first goal in a 3–1 win over

Bryan Hamilton

Blackburn Rovers. He appeared in two FA Cup finals for the Blues in consecutive years – in the first in 1906, when Newcastle United were beaten 1–0, he became one of just three amateurs this century to take an FA Cup winners' medal. He left Goodison Park in 1908, having scored 29 goals in 156 league and Cup games, to join Manchester United. He won four caps for England during his time with Everton, and an Olympic Games soccer gold medal with Great Britain in 1908. When he retired from playing, he became one of the game's great administrators. A solicitor by profession, he was a director of Manchester United for almost 50 years and chairman from 1951 until his death in 1965.

HARPER, ALAN. Alan Harper began his career with Liverpool but after five seasons of Central League football with the Anfield club he joined Everton in the summer of 1983 for a fee of £100,000. Despite being on the bench when the Blues won the FA Cup in 1984, this fine utility player won league championship medals in both 1985 and 1987. He had played in 167 league and Cup games for the club when, following the appointment of Colin Harvey as Everton manager, he was sold to Sheffield Wednesday for £275,000. It was a fairly traumatic 18 months for Harper at Hillsborough but his career was rescued by Howard Kendall in December 1989 when the former Everton boss took him to Manchester City. Harper was a firm favourite with the Maine Road crowd but it didn't stop him following Kendall back to Goodison in the summer of 1991 for £200,000 in a deal which also included another former Blue, Mark Ward. He played in another 60 league and Cup games before being given a free transfer at the end of the 1992–93 season. He had a season with Luton Town before joining Burnley in August 1994. After a good first season at Turf Moor, he found himself a fringe member of the Clarets' side, and following a loan spell with Cardiff City he returned to Burnley to join the coaching staff.

HARPER, JOE. Everton manager Harry Catterick paid Aberdeen £180,000 for Joe Harper – a Scottish League club record incoming fee – in December 1972. Despite missing a penalty on his debut in a 3–1 home win over Tottenham Hotspur, Harper's sharpness in and around the penalty area was in evidence from the start. At 5ft 6ins, Harper did not have the build to play in the style of Joe Royle, the injured striker he had been bought to replace, relying more on positional sense and timing. However, after only 14 months at Goodison he became homesick and returned to Scotland to play for Hibernian for a fee of £120,000, having scored 14 goals in 49 games for the Blues. In 1975, Harper was one of five Scotland players banned from international football following an incident in Copenhagen during Scotland's match with Denmark. A year later, he rejoined Aberdeen for £50,000 and was their leading scorer for three successive seasons before an injury ended his career.

HARRIS, BRIAN. One of the club's greatest utility players, Brian Harris played in every position except goalkeeper for the Everton first team. He was a winger when he joined the club from Port Sunlight in January 1954, but had to wait until August 1955 before making his first-team debut in a 1–0 win at Burnley. Over the next 12 seasons, he went on to appear in 358 league and Cup games, winning a league championship medal in 1962–63 and an FA Cup winners' medal in 1966 when he was one of the Blues' star players in the 3–2 win over Sheffield Wednesday. Best remembered as a defensive wing-half, he was a great favourite with the Goodison crowd. Therefore it came as a great surprise in October 1966 when he was allowed to join Cardiff City for £15,000. In

1967–68, he played in all nine of the Bluebirds' European Cup-Winners' Cup games when they just missed out on the final. He went on to appear in 148 league games for the Ninian Park club, later playing for and managing Newport County.

HARRIS, JIMMY. Birkenhead-born Jimmy Harris was a member of the district's successful schoolboy side before joining Everton as an amateur. He later turned professional and made his first-team debut in a 1–0 win at Burnley in August 1955, replacing Dave Hickson. Harris kept his place in the side, appearing in all 40 remaining games, and top-scoring with 19 league goals plus another four in the FA Cup. Midway through his first season with the club he won England Under-23 honours when he played against Scotland at Hillsborough. When Hickson, who had joined Aston Villa, returned to Goodison from his new club, Huddersfield Town, in the summer of 1957, Harris switched to outside-right but scored more goals than the former Everton favourite. In 1958–59, Harris scored a hat-trick in the match against Tottenham Hotspur at White Hart Lane but still ended up on the losing side as the Blues went down 10–4. In December 1960, after scoring 72 goals in 207 league and Cup games, he left Goodison to sign for Birmingham City for a 'substantial' fee. He scored 37 goals in 93 league games for the St Andrews club before ending his career with Oldham Athletic.

HARRIS, VAL. Valentine Harris was already an Irish international when he arrived at Goodison Park from Shelbourne in 1907, having won the first of his six caps at centre-forward. During his seven years with Everton, he went on to win a further 14 caps and showed his versatility by playing at wing-half, centre-half and inside-forward for his country. For Everton, the Dublin-born Harris played in six different positions, although the majority of his 214 first-team appearances were at right-half. Having made his debut at Woolwich Arsenal towards the end of the 1907–8 season, he became a key member of the Everton side which finished runners-up in the first division the following term. He collected another runners-up medal in 1911–12 as the Blues ended the season three points adrift of champions, Blackburn Rovers. After playing his last international match against Scotland in 1914, he returned to Shelbourne – Everton won the league championship the following season!

HARRISON, GEORGE. Born in Church Gresley, Derbyshire, George Harrison was a stocky winger who began his league career with Leicester Fosse. Three years later he joined Everton and made his debut in the Merseyside derby at Goodison Park which Liverpool won

2–1. Harrison was a dead-ball specialist and the majority of his 17 goals in his 190 appearances for the club came from free-kicks or the penalty spot. He was an excellent crosser of the ball and made many goals for his colleagues, especially Bobby Parker in 1914–15 when the former Rangers player scored 36 goals in 35 games as Everton won the league championship. During the First World War, Harrison scored ten goals in 46 games and when the football resumed after the hostilities his form was so impressive that he was capped twice by England. Early in the 1923–24 season, he moved to Preston North End and scored 75 goals in 274 league appearances for the Deepdale club before ending his career with Blackpool.

HART, HUNTER. Left-half Hunter Hart was signed from Airdrie for £4,000 in 1922 at a time when the Goodison Park club needed to strengthen their defence; they were struggling against relegation from the first division. The Blues lost 1–0 on his debut at Bolton Wanderers, but he held his place in the side and the club just avoided the drop into the second division. An ever-present in 1923–24, Hart went on to play in 300 league and Cup games for Everton and was a member of the team which helped Dixie Dean score his record-breaking 60 goals when they won the league championship in 1927–28. In 1929–30, the club were again struggling to avoid the drop but this time the Glasgow-born defender could not help them. Playing his last game in a 4–0 home win over Derby County on 18 January 1930, he was unable to hold down a regular place and retired shortly after making his final appearance.

HARTFORD, ASA. Born in Clydebank, Asa Hartford was plucked from Scottish amateur football after being spotted by a West Bromwich Albion scout, and signed professional forms for them in 1967. He was soon thrilling the crowds with his mature skill and vision and it was only a matter of time before the inevitable big-money offer arrived to tempt Albion. Hartford will probably always be remembered as the player whose transfer to first division giants, Leeds United, was sensationally called off after a routine medical examination revealed a hole-in-the-heart condition. That was in 1972 when he was poised to move from the Hawthorns to Elland Road for £170,000. Happily the condition was a minor one and in August 1974 he joined Manchester City for £225,000. He went on to play a major role in City's glorious era of the late 1970s, picking up a League Cup winners' medal with them in 1976. In June 1979, he signed for Nottingham Forest under the management of Brian Clough for £500,000 but after only 63 days and three league games he was on his way back to the north-west and

Asa Hartford

Everton. He made his debut for the Blues in a 1–1 home draw against Aston Villa. A wily character, quick of temper and determined, but also gifted, he was the kind of midfield terrier every successful team needs and in his first season at Goodison was voted Player of the Year by the supporters. Capped 50 times by Scotland, he later returned for a second spell with Manchester City before crossing the Atlantic to join Fort Lauderdale Sun. He returned to the top flight with Norwich City and helped them win the Milk Cup in 1985. He went on to play for Bolton Wanderers, was player-manager of Stockport County and managed Shrewsbury. He also worked for Blackburn and Stoke before returning to Maine Road for a third time as first-team coach.

HARVEY, COLIN. As a youngster, Colin Harvey had a trial with Liverpool and was told to report back the following week, but in the meantime he was invited for a trial at Goodison. He signed as an apprentice for the Blues in October 1962 and thereafter his progress was so rapid that within 11 months he had made his senior debut, deputising for the injured Jimmy Gabriel in a European Cup tie at Inter Milan's San Siro Stadium. Smoke bombs and fireworks along with the baying of over 90,000 Italians did not intimidate the 18-year-old Harvey. He played with maturity as the Blues lost by a single goal to one of the best club sides in the world. He established himself in the Everton side the following season, playing in a tough encounter with Manchester United. Two days later on 19 September 1964 he played in his first Merseyside derby; Everton won 4–0 and Harvey got on the scoresheet. However, he wasn't a prolific scorer from midfield and even his best-remembered goal, the winner at Burnden Park in the 1966 FA Cup semi-final against Manchester United, was mis-hit, bobbling past Harry Gregg from 15 yards. One that did go some way towards balancing the books came on the afternoon of 1 April 1970 when Everton entertained West Bromwich Albion. Veering past two defenders, he cracked home a 25-yard piledriver that even had his colleagues gaping in amazement. Surprisingly, Harvey who had every attribute demanded of a modern midfielder, won only one England cap and that was in 1971 when Malta were beaten 1–0. He had played in 384 league and Cup games for the Blues when, in October 1974, he moved to Sheffield Wednesday for £70,000. Sadly, a nagging hip injury caught up with him and 13 months later he was forced to retire. Harvey was an enthusiastic character who always found time for youngsters. He took up coaching and turned out to be a natural. There is no doubt that he can take much of the credit for Everton's success in the mid-1980s, but he was not cut out to be a manager. When he succeeded Howard Kendall in the summer of 1987, he seemed almost reluctant to do so, perhaps knowing deep down that it was not the right role for him. The club reached the finals of both the FA Cup and Simod Cup in 1988–89, but lost both, to Liverpool and Nottingham Forest respectively. The 1989–90 season was another undistinguished affair with the club finishing a disappointing sixth in the first division. At the end of October 1990, Harvey was summoned to Goodison and told that he was to be dismissed. Six days later he returned as assistant manager following the appointment of Howard Kendall. He later left Goodison to become assistant manager to Graeme Sharp at Oldham Athletic before both former Blues resigned their posts in February 1997.

HAT-TRICK HEROES. Everton players have netted 160 hat-tricks in the Football League. Dixie Dean holds the record with 33; the next highest is Bobby Parker with seven. The club's first hat-trick in the Football League was scored by Archie McKinnon in the 6–2 win over Derby County on 27 October 1888. Fred Pickering made a sensational debut for the Blues on 14 March 1964, scoring three in a 6–1 win over Nottingham Forest. Tony Cottee also hit three on his debut for the club, against Newcastle United on the opening day of the 1988–89 season. Joe Clennell scored a hat-trick on the opening day of the 1914–15 season when the Blues defeated Tottenham Hotspur 3–1. There have been five occasions when two Everton players have scored hat-tricks in the same match. The first came in 1892–93 when Fred Geary and Alex Latta scored the goals in a 6–1 win over Derby County. Jimmy Settle and Jack Taylor hit three apiece in a 6–1 victory over Wolves on 7 September 1901 and Dixie Dean and Jimmy Stein each scored four goals in the 9–1 win over Plymouth Argyle during the 1930–31 season. Joe Royle hit four goals and David Johnson three in an 8–0 win over Southampton on 20 November 1971, whilst five goals from Bob Latchford and three from Martin Dobson helped the Blues beat Wimbledon 8–0 in a second-round League Cup tie. Jimmy Harris holds the rare distinction of scoring a hat-trick and still finishing up on the losing side. It happened on 11 October 1958 when Spurs beat Everton 10–4 at White Hart Lane.

HEATH, ADRIAN. Starting his career with his home-town club Stoke City, Adrian Heath appeared briefly during the Potters' second division promotion-winning season of 1978–79. He became a virtual fixture in the club's midfield the following season, replacing Howard Kendall, who had departed for Blackburn Rovers. His busy, energetic style brought him his first taste of international honours in April 1981 when he scored twice for England Under-21s against Romania in the UEFA championships. The following January, in the week of his 21st birthday, he was transferred to Everton for a Goodison Park record fee of £700,000. After making his debut in a 1–1 draw at home to Southampton, he became an automatic choice in the Everton midfield. He was the club's top scorer during 1983–84 with 18 league and Cup goals as the Blues beat Watford to win the FA Cup. In 1984–85, the Blues came within 90 minutes of an unprecedented treble of league championship, European Cup-Winners' Cup and FA Cup, although because of injury Heath played only a supporting role. Manchester United ended their hopes by beating them 1–0 in the FA Cup final. In 1987, the Goodison club won the league championship with Heath this time playing a key role alongside Trevor Steven. After scoring 89 goals in 293 games, Heath signed for Espanol of Barcelona but spent less than a season in Spain before returning for a short spell with Aston Villa. In February 1990, he joined Manchester City, linking up once more with Howard Kendall. He returned to Stoke in March 1992 but five months later joined Burnley. In his first season with the Clarets he netted 20 goals, easily the best of his league career. After the club were relegated, he accepted the position of assistant manager at Sheffield United but returned to Turf Moor in February 1996 as the new Burnley manager when Jimmy Mullen was relieved of his position. In the summer of 1997, Heath left Burnley to return to Goodison Park as first-team coach.

HICKSON, DAVE. Dave Hickson first attracted the attention of Everton manager Cliff Britton as a free-scoring teenager with non-league Ellesmere Port but, after crossing the Mersey to join the Goodison Park club in the summer of 1948, his progress was halted by National Service. Two years later, he returned to an Everton side that had been relegated to the second division. He made his league debut at Leeds United in September 1951 and soon claimed a regular place in the Blues line-up, linking effectively with John Willie Parker. Hickson earned himself a place in Everton folklore during the club's stirring run to the 1953 FA Cup semi-finals. In the fifth-round tie with Manchester United, he scored the winner after leaving the field to have five stitches put in a gashed eyebrow. He later reopened the wound with a header against the post. In the quarter-final at Villa Park, he scored the only goal of the game with a scorching drive from just inside the penalty area after starting the move near the halfway line. During the 1953–54 season, he scored 25 league goals, including a hat-trick in a 4–2 win at Stoke City, but after just one more season of top-flight football, he was sold to Aston Villa for £17,500. He failed to settle in the Midlands, and at Huddersfield Town, his next port of call, and in the summer of 1957 he returned to Goodison for a bargain £7,500. After taking his tally of goals in his two spells at the club to 111 in 243 league and Cup appearances, he was allowed to cross Stanley Park and join Liverpool. Twelve months later, he left Anfield and went into non-league football with Cambridge United. Though he later had a stint with Tranmere Rovers, there was never any doubt about where his heart lay – Dave Hickson was and is an Everton man through and through.

HIGGINS, MARK. Following in the footsteps of his father, John, who was a giant centre-half with Bolton Wanderers, Mark Higgins joined Everton straight from school. He won a record 19 England Schoolboy caps and made his Everton debut on 5 October 1976 in a 2–2 home draw against Manchester City. Good in the air, Higgins soon established himself in the heart of the Everton defence and after partnering Billy Wright, he teamed up with Kevin Ratcliffe and was made captain. Higgins was an integral part of a successful Everton defence for many years until he was sidelined with

Andy Hinchcliffe

a persistent groin injury. He was finally forced to quit but a hernia operation seemed to do the trick and after a two-year break, Ron Atkinson gave him a chance at Manchester United. He had appeared in 181 first-team games for the Goodison Park club and, though United handed over £60,000 insurance compensation after he had proved his fitness, he made only eight senior appearances for the Old Trafford side. He later enjoyed spells with Bury, Stoke City and Burnley but within two months of his arrival at Turf Moor, he hurt his back and hung up his boots.

HINCHCLIFFE, ANDY. Andy Hinchcliffe began his career with Manchester City and after making his league debut against Plymouth Argyle on 15 August 1987, missed just two matches in that first season. He played a prominent part in the club's promotion to the first division during the following year and scored five times from the left-back position. During the 1990 close season, he was transferred to Everton in exchange for Neil Pointon and a large cash adjustment in City's favour. He made his Everton debut in a 3–2 home defeat by Leeds United on the opening day of the 1990–91 season. Once regarded as one of the most promising left-backs in the country, Hinchcliffe was only an occasional performer in his early days at Goodison but when Joe Royle arrived in 1994, he was switched to a midfield role wide on the left and his game was transformed. His brilliant crossing and dead-ball play was a key to the Blues' FA Cup success in 1995. Hinchcliffe's form won him recognition at full international level when he played against Moldova. Unfortunately, he suffered a long-term injury and missed the latter half of the 1996–97 season. With Howard Kendall back at the helm at Goodison, Hinchcliffe left the club to join Sheffield Wednesday.

HOLT, JOHNNY. Nicknamed the 'Little Everton Devil' by Everton supporters, Johnny Holt joined the club from Bootle in 1888 in time for the first season of league football. He made his debut in the club's first-ever Football League game when they beat Accrington at home 2–1. One of the best centre-halfs of his day, he won the first of ten England caps against Wales in 1890, though his proudest moment at international level came two years later when England played Scotland at Ibrox. The Scottish journalists were convinced that their star player, Sandy McMahon, would run rings round Holt. In fact, the Everton defender marked the Scottish forward out of the game in a 4–1 victory for England. Powerful in the air and one of the best man-to-man markers, Johnny Holt played in 252 league and Cup games in ten seasons with the Goodison Park club before leaving to end his career with Reading.

HOME MATCHES. Not including the club's pre-Football League matches, Everton's best home win is the 11–2 defeat of Derby County in a first-round FA Cup match on 18 January 1890. In the Football League, the Blues' best home wins are the 9–1 victories over Manchester City in a first division match on 3 September 1906 and Plymouth Argyle in a second division match on 27 December 1930. Everton have scored eight goals in a home match on seven occasions. They beat Stoke 8–0 on 2 November 1889 and repeated the scoreline against Southampton on 20 November 1971 and Wimbledon on 29 August 1978, the latter being in a League Cup tie. Darwen and Sheffield Wednesday were beaten 8–1 in the 1893–94 season, Plymouth Argyle 8–4 in 1953–54 and Cardiff City 8–3 in 1961–62. The club's worst home defeat occurred on Boxing Day 1933 when they went down 7–3 to Newcastle United, whilst the highest scoring match at Goodison Park other than those mentioned above is the Blues' 7–3 victory over Burnley on 27 December 1890.

HOME SEASONS. Everton have gone through a complete league season with an undefeated home record on just one occasion. In 1962–63, the Blues won 14 and drew seven of their 21 home matches when winning the first division championship. The club's highest number of home wins in a league season is 18 in 1931–32 (when they won the first division title) and 1967–68 (when they finished fifth in the first division).

HONOURS. The major honours achieved by the club are:

First division championship	1890–91	1914–15	1927–28
	1931–32	1938–39	1969–70
	1984–85	1986–87	
Runners-up	1889–90	1894–95	1901–02
	1904–05	1908–09	1911–12
	1985–86		
Second division championship	1930–31		
Runners-up	1953–54		
FA Cup winners	1906	1933	1966
	1984	1995	
Runners-up	1893	1897	1907
	1968	1985	1986
	1989		
League Cup runners-up	1976–77	1983–84	
FA Charity Shield winners	1928	1932	1963
	1970	1984	1985
	1987	1995	1986 (shared)
European Cup-Winners' Cup	1985		
FA Youth Cup winners	1965	1984	
Runners-up	1961	1977	1983

HORNE, BARRY. A late starter in league football, Barry Horne completed a chemistry degree at Liverpool University while playing as a part-timer for Rhyl in the Northern Premier League. On leaving university, he joined fourth division Wrexham and made his debut at Swindon Town in August 1984. During three years at the Racecourse Ground he missed just two games, so it came as no surprise when he moved to a bigger club, signing for Portsmouth. During his first season with the Fratton Park club, he made his first appearance for the Welsh team in a European championship qualifier against Denmark. He had made 79 league and Cup appearances for Pompey when Southampton paid £700,000 to take the Welshman to The Dell, making him the club's most expensive signing. He very rarely missed a game for the Saints but was most unexpectedly snapped up by Everton during the summer of 1992. Adding steel to the Goodison club's midfield, he scored on his debut in a 1–1 home draw against Sheffield Wednesday. With spirited performances and great leadership qualities, he proved to be an astute buy, yet after making 148 league and Cup appearances for the Blues, he was allowed to join Birmingham City in the summer of 1996 for £250,000 – somewhat surprising for a man who has won 54 Welsh caps.

HUNDRED GOALS. Everton have scored more than 100 league goals in a season on three occasions. The highest total is 121 goals scored in 1930–31 when they won the second division championship. In 1931–32, they scored 116 goals in winning the first division championship in their first season back in the top flight; and in 1927–28, they scored 102 goals when again the club won the first division title.

HURST, JOHN. Arriving at Goodison in a blaze of publicity in May 1962, the 14-year-old England Schoolboy international was converted from a centre-forward to a defensive wing-half, and after a number of outstanding displays during the club's 1965 FA Youth Cup success, he made his league debut as a substitute in a 1–1 draw at Stoke City in August 1965. No doubt helped by his early experience as a forward, Hurst prospered at the back and was one of the finest uncapped wing-halves in the country. Hurst was comfortable in possession and an intelligent reader of the game who was more likely to make a perceptive interception than be forced into a desperate challenge. In 1968, he confounded medical experts who said that he would not play again that season after contracting hepatitis on the eve of the FA Cup semi-final against Leeds United. Yet against all odds, he recovered in time to take his place in the final against West Bromwich Albion. Hurst was an ever-present for the next two seasons, including the championship-winning campaign of 1969–70. He went on to score 34 goals in 399 league and Cup games but in the summer of 1976 he was allowed to join Oldham Athletic. He had lost his place in the Everton side as Billy Bingham sought unsuccessfully to build a new side capable of emulating the triumphs of the Harry Catterick era. One of the game's most polished central defenders, Hurst spent five enjoyable and effective seasons at Boundary Park, appearing in 170 league games before retiring in 1981. The quietest man in the Everton dressing-room, 'Gentleman Jack', as he was known, was a most respected and impeccable professional who always let his football do the talking.

HUSBAND, JIMMY. Unorthodox winger Jimmy Husband was born in Newcastle and played his early football with north-east side Shields. Signed in the summer of 1963, the likeable Geordie was nicknamed 'Skippy' by Everton fans because of his running style. He made his debut for the Blues in a 1–1 draw at Fulham in April 1965 and the following season made his European debut as a 17-year-old in the 2–1 second-round second-leg win over Ujpest Dozsa. In 1968–69, he was the club's second-top scorer with 19 goals in 36 league games and the following campaign was a regular member of Everton's league championship-winning side. He won England Under-23 honours and was on the verge of the full international side a number of times, but was never selected. In November 1973, after scoring 55 goals in 197 first-team games, he left Everton to join Luton Town, where he made 143 league appearances over the next five seasons.

I

INTER-CITIES FAIRS CUP. For their opening game in the competition on 24 October 1962, Everton drew Scottish opposition in the shape of Dunfermline Athletic. The Blues won the first leg 1–0 with Dennis Stevens the scorer but lost the return game 2–0 and were out of Europe at the first hurdle. In 1964–65 they travelled to Norway to face Valerengen and won 5–2. A fortnight later, the Blues won 4–2 to qualify for the second round. Travelling north of the border, this time to play Kilmarnock, the Blues had no trouble in establishing a 2–0 first leg lead. In the second leg, Fred Pickering scored two goals in a 4–1 win. In round three, the Blues drew Manchester United who were riding high in the first division, but a superb rearguard action at Old Trafford gave the Blues a 1–1 draw. Sadly, in the return game goals from Connelly and Herd exploited the gaps left by defenders and United won 2–1. The following season, the Blues travelled to West Germany, where they secured a 1–1 draw with 1FC Nurnburg, thanks to a Brian Harris goal. In the return, Jimmy Gabriel scored the only goal of the game to put Everton into the next round. Playing against Ujpest Dozsa, they went down 3–0 and though they gained some revenge with a 2–1 win at Goodison, it wasn't enough to put them into the next round.

INTERNATIONAL MATCHES. Goodison Park has been host to 11 full international matches involving England. The first was on 6 April 1895 when Everton's Johnny Holt was a member of the England side that beat Scotland 3–0. It was another 12 years before Goodison was the venue for an international match, with Everton's Harold Hardman scoring the only goal of the game in a 1–0 win over Ireland on 16 February 1907. The third international match to be played at Goodison saw Scotland's last visit to the ground. With no Everton players in their side, England drew 1–1. Between 1924 and 1953, Northern Ireland played five international matches at Goodison. On 22 October 1924, Everton's Sam Chedgzoy created all three England goals in a 3–1 win; four years later, Dixie Dean scored England's winner in a 2–1 victory. Everton's Cliff Britton was in the England side of 1935 when two goals from Arsenal's Cliff Bastin gave the home side a 2–1 win. The fourth of these matches, played on 5 November 1947, was a fiercely fought encounter that ended in a 2–2 draw. Six years later, England met Northern Ireland in a World Cup qualifier at Goodison with Bolton's forwards Hassall (2) and Lofthouse scoring the goals in a 3–1 win for England. On 21 September 1949, Everton's Peter Farrell and Tommy Eglington were in the Republic of Ireland side that triumphed 2–0 at Goodison Park, the first country other than the home nations to win on English soil. On 19 May 1951, England defeated Portugal 5–2. The last international match involving England at Goodison Park took place on 5 January 1966 when a Bobby Moore goal gave the home side a 1–1 draw against Poland. Goodison Park staged five games in the 1966 World Cup and the Brazil v Japan game in 1995.

INTERNATIONAL PLAYERS. The club's most capped player (i.e. caps gained while players were registered with Everton) is Neville Southall with 91 caps for Wales. The following is a complete list of players who have gained full international honours whilst at Goodison Park.

England		*Scotland*	
W. Abbott	1	J. Bell	8
B.H. Baker	2	G. Brewster	1
A.J. Ball	39	R.J. Collins	6
W. Balmer	1	J. Conolly	1
T. Booth	1	J. Dunn	1
W. Boyes	2	D. Ferguson	3
P. Bracewell	3	J. Gabriel	2
C.S. Britton	9	T. Gillick	5
E. Chadwick	7	A. Gray	1
S. Chedgzoy	8	A. Hartford	7
W. Cresswell	1	N. McBain	2
J.N. Cunliffe	1	A. Parker	1

England		Scotland	
W.R. Dean	16	B.D. Rioch	6
M. Dobson	1	J.T. Robertson	1
R.W. Downs	1	A.S. Scott	5
B.C. Freeman	2	G. Sharp	12
F. Geary	2	J.R. Thomson	1
C.W. Gee	3	A. Troup	1
A. Geldard	4	G.W. Wilson	1
H.P. Hardman	4	G. Wood	3
G. Harrison	2	A. Young	2
J.C. Harvey	1	A.(S.) Young	2
A. Hinchcliffe	3		
J. Holt	9	*Northern Ireland*	
R.H. Howarth	1	W.P. Bingham	12
F. Jefferis	2	D. Clements	12
T.C.F. Johnson	3	W. Cook	12
A.H. Kay	1	J. Coulder	5
B.L. Labone	26	T.J. Eglington	6
R.D. Latchford	12	P.D. Farrell	7
T. Lawton	8	B. Hamilton	11
G. Lineker	11	V. Harris	14
H. Makepeace	4	M.J. Hill	3
J. Mercer	5	J. Houston	3
A. Milward	4	R.W. Irvine	11
K.R. Newton	8	T. Jackson	6
F. Pickering	3	W. Lacey	10
P. Reid	13	P.W. Scott	2
J. Royle	2	W. Scott	16
E. Sagar	4	J. Sheridan	5
J. Settle	3	A.E. Stevenson	14
J. Sharp	2		
T. Steven	25	*Wales*	
G. Stevens	26	S. Arridge	3
D.W. Temple	1	J. Davies	2
D. Unsworth	1	S. Davies	3
D. Watson	6	W.D. Davies	16
G, West	3	T.P. Griffiths	8
T.A White	1	E. Hughes	2
R. Wilson	33	J.V. Humphreys	1
S. Wolstenholme	1	R.S. Jones	1
T.J. Wright	11	T.G. Jones	17

THE GOODISON PARK ENCYCLOPEDIA

Republic of Ireland		Wales		
T.J. Clinton	3	C.F. Parry	6	
P.J. Corr	4	A. Powell	2	
D. Donovan	5	K. Ratcliffe	58	
T.J. Eglington	22	L.R. Roose	2	
P.D. Farrell	26	D.P. Smallman	4	
J. McDonagh	3	N. Southall	91	
M.K. Meagan	4	G. Speed	7	
E. O'Keefe	1	M. Thomas	1	
J.A. O'Neill	17	P. Van Den Hauwe		13
K. Sheedy	38	R.T. Vernon	13	
M.A. Walsh	1	B.D. Williams	6	
M. Walsh	4			

IRVINE, ALAN. Signed as an amateur from Queen's Park in May 1981, Alan Irvine was an old-fashioned type of winger who had superb close control and great dribbling ability. He made his debut for the Blues in a 2–0 home win over Aston Villa in December 1981 and went on to play in the remaining 25 games of that campaign. However, the following season he failed to produce his earlier form and struggled to hold down a first-team place. Not happy with playing reserve-team football, he asked for a transfer at the beginning of the 1983–84 season. Manager Howard Kendall turned down his request and Irvine went on to appear in 38 league and Cup games that season including the Milk Cup final games against Liverpool. He played in the seven FA Cup games leading up to the final against Watford but failed to win a place on the day. He had appeared in 80 games over his three seasons with the club before being allowed to join Crystal Palace in the summer of 1984 for £50,000. After 109 league games for the Selhurst Park club he returned to Scotland to play for Dundee United, eventually signing for Blackburn Rovers in 1989.

IRVINE, BOBBY. Able to play in any of the forward positions, Bobby Irvine joined Everton from Dunmurry in September 1921 and made his debut in the Merseyside derby a couple of months later. That season he scored 11 goals in 25 league games, including hat-tricks against Aston Villa (home 3–2) and Huddersfield Town (home 6–2). He found the net 57 times in 214 appearances for the club. Not a prolific goalscorer, he was a superb dribbler of the ball and created many chances for Dixie Dean. He won his first cap for Northern Ireland against Scotland in March 1922 and during his six and a half seasons at Goodison was capped 11 times. He was in the Irish teams that beat England in 1923 and 1927, and at Anfield in 1926 he scored against the home side in a 3–3 draw. He left Everton after nine games of the club's 1927–28 league championship-winning season to sign for Portsmouth. He later played for Connah's Quay and then Derry City where he won the last of his 15 international caps, almost ten years after he had won his first.

J

JACKSON, GEORGE. Full-back George Jackson was spotted by Everton while he was playing for Walton Parish Church. He worked his way through the club's ranks, playing the occasional game on loan for Marine. He was in the Crosby side's team when they met Dulwich Hamlet in the FA Amateur Cup final at Upton Park before returning to Goodison Park. He made his Everton debut in a 5–2 home win over Wolverhampton Wanderers on 9 February 1935, soon establishing himself as a first-team regular. Playing for the club on both sides of the Second World War, he played in 79 league and Cup games before joining Caernarvon Town in 1949.

JEFFERIS, FRANK. Frank Jefferis was playing for Fordingbridge Turks when he was invited to Southampton in March 1905 and scored three goals in a reserve game. The following month he played for the Saints against the Corinthians and scored another hat-trick. He soon gained a regular place in the Southampton side and in six seasons with the club scored 48 goals in 170 Southern League appearances. He moved to Goodison Park in March 1911 and within a year had won two England caps. In 1914–15, he assisted Everton in winning the league championship. After wartime football with Everton, he played for them for half a season when the game resumed but in January 1920 signed for Preston North End. Two years later he was a member of their beaten FA Cup final side. In 1923 he was appointed player-coach of Southport, although after two seasons he hung up his boots to concentrate on the coaching. In 1927 he was forced back into action and played in a couple of games when Southport were short of players.

David Johnson

In 1936 he joined Millwall as their trainer and remained there until his death two years later.

JOHNSON, DAVID. David Johnson joined Everton in 1969, but despite scoring 15 goals in 58 appearances, including a hat-trick in an 8–0 win over Southampton, he was allowed to join Ipswich Town in 1972. Whilst at Portman Road he won the first of his eight full international caps for England when he played against Wales in 1975, but in the summer of 1976 he left Ipswich after scoring 46 goals in 178 league and Cup appearances, to become Liverpool's first £200,000 signing. Not helped by a succession of injuries, he managed only glimpses of his best form and although he collected a title medal and figured in the Wembley defeat by Manchester United, he missed out on European glory. He won a second league championship medal in 1979–80 but in August 1982 after netting 78 goals in 204 games, he returned to Everton for £100,000. His second spell with the club was little short of a disaster as his goal touch was missing. He spent a month on loan at Barnsley before joining Manchester City. A brief spell with NASL side Tulsa Roughnecks followed and he ended his Football League career with Preston North End. David Johnson occupies a unique place in Merseyside folklore – he is the only man to score a derby winner for both Everton and Liverpool.

JOHNSON, TOMMY. Tommy Johnson, 'Tosh' to his colleagues and supporters, spent 11 seasons with Manchester City between 1919 and 1930 and scored a total of 166 league and Cup goals for the club. In fact, he still holds the club's record for the most goals in a single season. His 38 goals in 1928–29, City's first season back in the top flight, is the best ever by a Maine Road player. He won two England caps, played in the 1926 FA Cup final and helped City win promotion in 1927–28. In addition, he played for the Football League and FA XI. He was nearly 30 when City released him in March 1930, transferring him to Everton for £6,000. It wasn't the most popular of decisions and there were plenty of City supporters who criticised the club for letting him go. Making his Everton debut in a 1–0 defeat at Newcastle United, he proved to be the perfect foil for the stunning power of Dixie Dean. His only hat-trick for the club came on 27 December 1932 in a 6–1 home win over Blackburn Rovers. At the end of that season, Johnson was outstanding in an Everton side that defeated Manchester City 3–0 in the FA Cup final. In a successful career, he won three more caps for England whilst with Everton and collected first and second division championship medals.

JONES, GARY. One of the most controversial players ever to wear the Everton shirt, Gary Jones made his league debut for the Blues in a 3–0 home win over Coventry City in April 1971, seven months after illness prevented him from playing in a European Cup tie against Keflavik. He had to wait until his 36th game for the club before scoring his first goal in a 1–1 draw at home to Chelsea in October 1974. A great crosser of the ball, he created many of Bob Latchford's goals, but in February 1986, after the Blues had lost 3–0 at Manchester City, he submitted a transfer request. The Goodison board had no hesitation in turning it down as Jones was extremely popular with the Everton faithful. However, a month later, the Huyton-born player was suspended for a fortnight after making a gesture to the bench when substituted in a match against Leeds United. At the end of that season he left Goodison to join Birmingham City but after just 33 appearances for the St Andrews side he went to play in the NASL with Fort Lauderdale.

JONES, JACK. Full-back Jack Jones started his career as a centre-forward. In his days with Ellesmere Port Town, from whom Everton signed him, he played alongside the great Joe Mercer. His first game in Everton colours came in a 2–0 home win over Leeds United towards the end of the 1933–34 season. His appearances the following season were limited, but he became an automatic choice in 1935–36 and missed only a few odd games due to injury over the next three seasons.

One of the game's most reliable defenders, Jones appeared in 108 games for the club, the only blot on his Goodison career being his dismissal during the final match of Everton's tour of Denmark in 1937. The Bebington-born player later ended his career with Sunderland.

JONES, TOMMY E. Everton's first-choice centre-half throughout the 1950s, Tommy Jones signed professional forms after successfully captaining the England and Liverpool County FA Youth teams. Originally, he was a full-back but Cliff Britton recognised his potential and converted him into a centre-half when the Blues needed a replacement for his namesake, Tommy G. Jones. He made his first-team debut in a 2–1 defeat at Arsenal in September 1950. Although Tommy Jones was a strong tackler and powerful in the air, excelling in clashes with Bolton and England centre-forward Nat Lofthouse, he lacked the streak of ruthlessness that runs through most top defenders. Full international honours surprisingly eluded him, but he did play for an England XI against the British Army at Maine Road and captained the FA side that toured Ghana and Nigeria in the summer of 1958. A cool converter of penalty kicks, he became club captain on Peter Farrell's departure in 1957. Eventually the slowness on the turn which had always been in evidence grew more marked and after David Herd had netted four times for Arsenal in a 6–1 win at Goodison in September 1958, he was replaced by the young Brian Labone. His career came to an end after he smashed a knee-cap in a Central League game at Barnsley. In the early 1960s he left Britain to coach in Italy.

JONES, TOMMY G. Tommy Jones joined Everton from Wrexham, for whom he had made just seven first-team appearances, in March 1936 for a fee of £3,000. A footballing centre-half, he made his debut for the Blues six months later in a 1–0 defeat at Leeds United but it was his only game of the season. Jones established himself in the Everton side the following campaign, at the end of which he won the first of his 17 Welsh caps when he played against Northern Ireland. During the war years he appeared in 142 games for the club and when league football resumed in 1946–47, he was again the club's first-choice pivot. He scored his first league goal for the club in a 3–2 defeat at Sheffield United. In the summer of 1949, he was appointed the club captain but a year earlier he could have joined Italian giants AS Roma who made several desperate attempts to sign him. Towards the end of his Goodison career he upset the Everton board by expressing his concern about the way the club was being run and left to join Pwllheli as player-manager.

K

KANCHELSKIS, ANDREI. The Ukrainian-born winger joined Manchester United in May 1991 from the Soviet club Shakhytor Donetsk. He left his country following the fall of communism. At Old Trafford, Kanchelskis was a key member of the United double-winning side of 1994. He also won a Premier League title medal in 1993 and a Coca-Cola Cup winners' medal in 1992. He scored a hat-trick for United against Manchester City in the Reds' 5–0 Old Trafford win over their local rivals in November 1994. It was the first hat-trick in a Manchester derby game for 33 years. The lightning-fast winger's £5 million move to Everton was one of the most drawn-out transfers in the history of the game and led to a souring of relations between the two clubs. In fact, the saga dragged on so long that Kanchelskis missed the start of the 1995–96 season. Nevertheless, he still finished the campaign as top scorer at Goodison Park with 17 goals, including a breathtaking end of season hat-trick in a 5–2 win over Sheffield Wednesday. His debut in September 1995, ironically against Manchester United, was one of the most painful on record as the Russian international was tackled by Lee Sharpe after just 14 minutes and dislocated his shoulder. He went on to score 22 goals in 60 games for the Blues before leaving to join Fiorentina for £8 million. In July 1998, he joined Glasgow Rangers for £5.5 million.

KAY, TONY. Beginning his career with Sheffield Wednesday, red-haired Tony Kay made his first-team debut in 1954 but didn't become a regular until the arrival of manager Harry Catterick four years later. He played in seven England Under-23 matches and represented the

Football League on three occasions. An ever-present for the Owls in 1960–61 and 1961–62, he went on to play in 203 league and Cup games before signing for Everton in December 1962 for a then record fee for a half-back of £55,000. He made his debut for the Blues in a 3–1 defeat at Leicester City but it wasn't long before manager Catterick appointed him captain and he went on to play a leading role in the club's league championship-winning success of 1962–63. In 1963 he won his one and only England cap when he scored in the 8–1 win over Switzerland in Zurich. In 1965 he was at the centre of the game's greatest-ever scandal, when he was sent to prison and banned for life after the infamous soccer bribes trial. It was a very sad end to the career of a man who was one of the most talented wing-halves of his day.

KELLY, THEO. Everton's first-ever manager, Theo Kelly, had been club secretary for a number of years when it was decided to offer him the newly created post. Although he was a fine administrator, the Everton players found him both difficult and uncommunicative. Kelly was appointed at the end of the 1938–39 season, after the club had won the league championship for the fifth time. His first seven seasons in charge found him managing an Everton side playing in wartime regional football but when league football did resume, he angered the Goodison fans by selling Tommy Lawton to Chelsea. Also Joe Mercer found it difficult to play under Kelly and left to play for Arsenal. As a manager, Kelly did not believe in buying players, arguing that they should mature through the club's nursery team rather than the chequebook! With the club hovering just above the relegation zone, his term of office came to an end in 1948 when he reverted to his former position of secretary.

KELSO, BOB. Scottish international Bob Kelso first made his name with Renton when they were one of the top teams north of the border. In the close season of 1888 he moved to Newcastle West End but within a few months he had joined Everton. He made his debut against Preston North End towards the end of the club's first season in the Football League. He then left Everton to play for Preston North End and in two seasons with the Deepdale club, made 38 league appearances. Kelso was a fine defender, completely at home at full-back as well as wing-half. In the summer of 1891 he rejoined Everton. He was a member of the side which lost to Wolverhampton Wanderers in the 1893 FA Cup final at Fallowfield and he was an important member of the side that ended the 1894–95 season as runners-up in the first division. He played in 103 first-team games for Everton before joining Dundee in the 1896 close season, winning further international caps.

Howard Kendall

KENDALL, HOWARD. Howard Kendall became the youngest player ever to appear in an FA Cup final when he played at left-half for Preston North End against West Ham United in 1964 just 20 days before his 18th birthday. After making 104 appearances for North End, he signed for Everton for £80,000 in March 1967. He was pitched straight into top-flight action two days later for the home match with Southampton and endured a traumatic 90 minutes, missing an open goal and looking completely out of his depth. But there was no doubting the ability of the former England Youth captain and he went on to be part of the most influential midfield combination Everton has ever had. Along with Alan Ball and Colin Harvey he ran the side's engine room as the club swept to an emphatic championship success in 1969–70. Kendall was very unlucky never to win full England recognition and was widely regarded as his country's most accomplished uncapped performer. Not a prolific scorer from midfield, he did chip in with his share of crucial goals, such as the winner in the

Merseyside derby at Goodison in February 1968 and a European Cup equaliser against Borussia Moenchengladbach in October 1970. However, perhaps Kendall's most spectacular strike came in the FA Cup quarter-final of 1968 at Filbert Street when he capped an outstanding personal display in the Blues' 3–1 win by hitting home a waist-high volley following a slick interchange of passes initiated by himself. After playing in 274 league and Cup games for the club, Kendall left Goodison Park to join Birmingham City in February 1974 as part of a complicated £350,000 deal which brought Bob Latchford to Everton. In August 1977, he was transferred to Stoke City and despite being tempted by an offer from North American side Minnesota Kicks, he became club coach under Alan Durban in 1978. He then became player-manager at Blackburn Rovers and having taken the Ewood Park club from the third division to the brink of the first division, he was ready for the big-time. On 8 May 1981, Kendall returned to the scene of his greatest triumphs. Only days after his arrival he made his objectives perfectly clear – he wanted to win a trophy, something the club had failed to do since he was a member of the 1969–70 championship-winning side. Two years later the club's trophy cabinet was still bare and a section of the crowd wanted Kendall out. Then it happened – a Milk Cup quarter-final at Oxford United was drifting away when Adrian Heath latched on to a dreadful back-pass to snatch a late equaliser. Everton won the replay and were off and running. They met Liverpool in the Milk Cup final and beat Watford in the FA Cup final. The following season brought the first league title in 15 years, a first European trophy and glorious failure in the FA Cup final against Manchester United. Howard Kendall was named Manager of the Year. After winning the league championship again in 1986–87, Kendall felt he could do no more and joined Spanish club Atletico Bilbao. After two happy and successful years he left by mutual consent and on his return to England was appointed manager of Manchester City. He had been in charge at Maine Road for less than 12 months when he sensationally resigned to return to Goodison following the sacking of Colin Harvey. He stayed with the club until December 1993 when he resigned after watching his side gain their first Premiership victory at home for ten weeks. He had spells in charge at Notts County and Sheffield United before becoming manager of Everton for a third time in June 1997. At the end of the 1997–98 season, Kendall parted company with the club again following a season in which the club hung on to their Premiership status on goal difference from Bolton Wanderers.

KENYON, ROGER. Seen as the natural replacement for long-serving international centre-half Brian Labone, Roger Kenyon made his Everton debut in a 2–2 draw at Arsenal in November 1967 and went on to play his early games for the club alongside the Everton captain. He was substitute but did not play in the club's FA Cup final side of 1968, and he made nine appearances in the league championship-winning season of 1969–70. Towards the end of that campaign, his performances earned him some glowing tributes and, from then on, he became the club's first-choice pivot. The team's performances went into decline, and Kenyon's career wasn't helped when he was badly injured in a car crash in 1974. Despite being constantly plagued by a series of niggling injuries, he was an England substitute for the European championship games against West Germany, Cyprus and Wales at Wembley the following year. He stayed at Goodison until midway through the 1978–79 season but then, having played in 306 league and Cup games, he left to play for Vancouver Whitecaps, whom he steered to the NASL title in his first year.

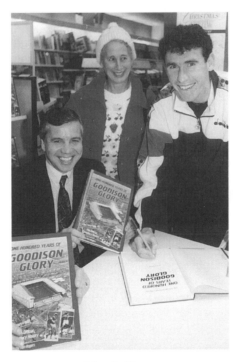

Martin Keown

KEOWN, MARTIN. Oxford-born Martin Keown began his career with Arsenal. In 1984–85 he gained experience while on loan with Brighton and Hove Albion and returned to Highbury to make his Arsenal league debut at West Bromwich Albion. However, following a contract dispute he was transferred to Aston Villa for £125,000 in the summer of 1986. Keown spent just over three years at Villa Park, playing in almost 150 first-team games and winning eight England Under-21 caps. In August 1989, he was transferred to Everton for £750,000, making his debut in a 1–1 draw at Sheffield Wednesday. After taking a while to settle in, Keown established himself as a first-team regular and in 1991–92 won the first of his 15 England caps when he played against France. In February 1993, George Graham paid Everton £2 million to take Keown back to Highbury, where he is still the club's leading utility player.

KIDD, BRIAN. Brian Kidd joined Manchester United as a schoolboy and made his debut in the Charity Shield against Tottenham Hotspur at Old Trafford in August 1967. From that moment on he was a regular choice, and on his 19th birthday he achieved everlasting fame when he scored United's third goal in the 4–1 European Cup final victory over Benfica at Wembley. He was capped twice by England, winning both caps in 1970, appearing against Northern Ireland and Ecuador. He scored 70 goals in 264 league and Cup games for Manchester United before being transferred to Arsenal in the summer of 1974 for £110,000. He went on to score 30 goals in 77 league appearances for the Gunners, a scoring rate which tempted Manchester City to pay £100,000 to bring him back north. He finished his first season at Maine Road as top scorer with 21 goals and topped the charts 12 months later with 16. In March 1979 he was on the move again as Everton paid £150,000 for his services. He made his debut in a 3–1 defeat at Bolton Wanderers and although he never recaptured his form of the 1970s, he did end the 1979–80 season as the club's top scorer with ten goals. In May 1980 he moved to Bolton Wanderers, hanging up his boots after scoring 16 goals in 49 games. In 1991 he was appointed assistant manager of Manchester United.

KING, ANDY. Signed by Billy Bingham from his home-town club Luton Town for £35,000 in April 1976, Andy King was idolised by Everton fans, who appreciated this hugely gifted player. He made his debut for the Blues in a 3–1 home win over Middlesbrough and, although he failed to score in that game, he did score a number of valuable goals for the club. In 1977–78 he was ever-present as the Blues finished third in Division One, his form almost bringing him full international honours. In September 1980 he joined Queens Park Rangers for £450,000 but

Andy King

after just one year at Loftus Road he moved to West Bromwich Albion for a similar fee. King just could not live without Everton and in the summer of 1982 he returned to Goodison for a second spell. Sadly, he failed to realise his full potential and after scoring 68 goals in 247 league and Cup games in his two spells with the club, he was allowed to leave and went to play for Dutch side Cambuur. He later returned to England to play for Wolverhampton Wanderers, Luton Town and Aldershot before entering management with Mansfield Town.

L

LABONE, BRIAN. Brian Labone was one of the greatest players to wear the royal blue of Everton. He won every honour in the game, including 26 England caps, and captained the club for seven years. He made his Everton debut at Birmingham City in March 1958 but on his home debut he was given a chasing by Spurs' Bobby Smith as the Blues lost 4–3 with the young Labone responsible for three of the goals. He was dropped. The following season, when Tommy E. Jones was injured, Labone was recalled and, apart from being left out just once more, he stayed in the side until 1971 when an Achilles injury ended his career. During the 1962–63 season, he became the first Evertonian to be capped by England since the war and was a huge influence on the club's league championship-winning campaign. After holding aloft the FA Cup in 1966, he asked to be excused from England's World Cup party to concentrate on his wedding plans, and in 1967 astounded the whole of the soccer world by announcing his retirement! Having lost both form and confidence, Labone told the club that he would part company with them in 18 months' time or as soon as a suitable replacement was found, to enable him to enter the family business. Thankfully, this dramatic move cleared his mind and he soon returned to peak form. Alf Ramsey continued to select him at international level and so he reversed his decision. In 1969–70 he helped Everton to another league championship and excelled for England in the subsequent World Cup finals. After injuring an Achilles tendon in a Central League game in September 1971, he was forced to quit the game the following year. He had made 530 league and Cup appearances for the Blues. Honoured at Goodison both as a

Brian Labone

loyal and distinguished player, he was, as Harry Catterick once called him, 'the last of the great Corinthians'.

LARGEST CROWD. Goodison Park housed its largest crowd for the derby match against Liverpool on 18 September 1948. A crowd of 78,299 saw the Blues draw 1–1, Ephraim Dodds scoring for the home side.

LATCHFORD, BOB. A big, bustling centre-forward, Bob Latchford made his name with his home-town club Birmingham City, for whom he scored 68 goals in 160 league appearances. He signed for Everton in February 1974 for a fee of £350,000 and made his debut in a 4–3 defeat at West Ham United. In his first four full seasons with the Goodison club, Latchford was the top league goalscorer, reaching his peak in

Bob Latchford

1977–78 when he became the first Division One player for six years to reach the 30-goal mark. His total included four in a 5–1 win at Queens Park Rangers. Latchford reached the final game of that 1977–78 season, at home to Chelsea, needing two goals to claim a national newspaper prize of £10,000. Everton won 6–0 and Latchford netted the goals necessary to win the money and carve a place for himself in Merseyside football folklore. Whilst at Goodison, Latchford won 12 full international caps for England, the first against Italy in 1977. In the summer of 1981, after scoring 138 goals in 289 league and Cup games, he left to join Swansea City for £125,000. He enjoyed mixed fortunes at Vetch Field, but he did score 32 goals in 1982–83 before being given a free transfer and joining Dutch club, Breda. Within five months he had returned to England and signed for Coventry City. Twelve months later, he left to play for Lincoln City, ending his league career with Newport County.

LATE FINISHES. Everton's final match of the season against Arsenal at Highbury on 31 May 1947 is the latest date for the finish of any Blues season. Arsenal won 2–1 with Tommy Eglington scoring for Everton. During the Second World War, many curious things occurred, among them the continuance of the 1940–41 season into June. Everton's last competitive match that campaign saw them play at home to Liverpool on 2 June. The Blues won 3–1 with tiny winger Wally Boyes scoring two of the goals and full-back George Jackson, playing at centre-forward, scoring the other.

LATTA, ALEX. Scottish international winger Alex Latta began his career with his home-town club Dumbarton Athletic before joining Everton in 1889. He made his debut in a 3–2 home win over Blackburn Rovers on the opening day of the 1889–90 season and over the next six seasons was the club's regular outside-right. Forming a formidable partnership with inside-forward Alec Brady, Latta, who was quite tall for a winger, scored his fair share of goals and hit hat-tricks against Notts County in 1889–90 (home 5–3), West Bromwich Albion in 1891–92 (home 4–3), Notts County in 1891–92 (home 4–0), Derby County in 1892–93 (away 6–1) and Small Heath in 1894–95 (away 4–4). On 19 October 1892, he scored all four of Everton's goals in a 4–3 win at Newton Heath. A member of the Everton side which won the league championship in 1890–91, he also appeared in the club's FA Cup final team of 1893. He retired from the game in 1896, having scored 70 goals in 148 league and Cup games for Everton.

LAWSON, DAVID. David Lawson became Britain's most expensive goalkeeper when he joined Everton from Huddersfield Town for £80,000 in the summer of 1972. Born in Wallsend, Lawson joined Newcastle United as an apprentice but after failing to make the first team, he was allowed to leave and joined Bradford Park Avenue. Even at the now defunct Yorkshire club, Lawson was not sure of a first-team place and in 1969 moved to Huddersfield Town. Replacing regular keeper Terry Poole, who had broken his leg, he went on to establish himself in the Terriers' side over the next three seasons, and had appeared in 51 league games before his move to Everton. He made his debut for the Blues in a 1–1 draw at Norwich City on the opening day of the 1972–73 season and went on to play in 38 league games during that campaign. In 1973–74, he was ever-present as Everton finished seventh in the first division but early the following season he lost his place through injury to Dai Davies. He regained his place at the start of the 1975–76 season and went on to play in 150 games for the club before being allowed to join Luton Town for £15,000 in October 1978. He later moved to Stockport County where he played in 118 games for the Edgeley Park club.

LAWTON, TOMMY. One of the greatest centre-forwards of all time, Tommy Lawton was born in Bolton and in three seasons of schoolboy football scored a staggering 570 goals. He joined Burnley as a groundstaff boy in 1934 and made his debut four days after his 17th birthday, scoring a hat-trick against Tottenham Hotspur. He had scored 11 goals in 18 games during the first half of the 1936–37 season when Everton paid £6,500 for the young Lawton in December 1936. He scored on his Everton debut but the Blues went down 7–2 at Wolverhampton Wanderers. At first, Lawton appeared at inside-forward to accommodate Dixie Dean but the following season he settled down at centre-forward. He was the club's top scorer in 1937–38 with 28 goals and in 1938–39 netted 34 goals in 38 league games plus another four in the FA Cup. That season Everton won the league championship and Lawton was the country's top league goalscorer, including all four in a 4–4 draw at Middlesbrough and a hat-trick in a 4–0 home win over the then Ayresome Park club. Lawton's four goals in the FA Cup all came in the fourth-round encounter with Doncaster Rovers which the Blues won 8–0. It was during this season that Lawton won the first of his 23 England caps when he played against Wales – all of this and he was still only 19 years old. After the war, Lawton became involved in a dispute with Everton which led to him being transferred to Chelsea in November 1945. He spent two years at Stamford Bridge before moving to Notts County for the then British record fee of £20,000. During his five seasons at Meadow Lane, he helped Notts County win promotion to the second division in 1949–50 as well as scoring 90 goals in 151 league appearances. His next move was to Brentford in March 1952 but after only 18 months he was transferred to Arsenal. Although in the twilight of his career, he scored 13 goals in 35 league games before joining Kettering Town as player-manager. He later managed Notts County, ending a playing career during which he had scored 231 league goals in 390 games for his six clubs, and 22 goals in 23 full England matches. If his wartime and Victory internationals are taken into account, his England figures are 46 goals in 45 games.

LEADING GOALSCORERS. Everton have provided the Football League's divisional leading goalscorer on 13 occasions. They are:

1893–94	Jack Southworth	Football League	27
1901–02	Fred Priest	first division	18
1906–07	Alex Young	first division	28
1908–09	Bertie Freeman	first division	36
1914–15	Bobby Parker	first division	36
1923–24	Wilf Chadwick	first division	28
1927–28	Dixie Dean	first division	60
1930–31	Dixie Dean	second division	39
1931–32	Dixie Dean	first division	45
1937–38	Tommy Lawton	first division	28
1938–39	Tommy Lawton	first division	34
1977–78	Bob Latchford	first division	30
1985–86	Gary Lineker	first division	30

LEAGUE GOALS – CAREER HIGHEST. Dixie Dean holds the Goodison Park record for the most league goals with a career total of 377 goals between 1924 and 1938.

LEAGUE GOALS – FEWEST CONCEDED. During the 1987–88 season, the Toffees conceded just 27 goals in finishing fourth in the first division.

LEAGUE GOALS – MOST INDIVIDUAL. Dixie Dean holds the Everton record for the most league goals in a season with 60 in 1927–28 when the Blues won the first division championship.

LEAGUE GOALS – MOST SCORED. Everton's highest goal tally in the Football League was during the club's second division championship winning season of 1930–31 when they scored 121 goals.

LEE, GORDON. Gordon Lee arrived at Goodison Park in 1977 with a reputation as a soccer troubleshooter. In his first managerial post, he took Port Vale up to the third division, and he won promotion for Blackburn Rovers during their centenary season of 1974–75. At Newcastle United, he steered the Magpies to the League Cup and into Europe. Passionately committed to the Everton cause, Lee took the Everton job with the Blues near the foot of the first division, although they were in the semi-final of the League Cup. By the end of the season, they had risen to ninth place, reached the semi-final of the FA Cup and lost the League Cup final, but only after two replays. Lee went on to build a side of considerable ability and one worth watching. In his first full season with the club they finished third and were the first division's highest scorers with 76 goals. The following season, 1977–78, the Blues went 19 games without defeat. Midway through the campaign, in which the club finished fourth in the first division, Lee was charged with bringing the game into disrepute after he criticised a referee for allowing a game to go ahead on a treacherous pitch at The Dell. He was later cleared by an FA disciplinary committee. Lee's forays into the transfer market failed to prevent a miserable slump and as confidence waned, so did attendances. The Everton fans grew disillusioned with his perplexing team permutations and, in May 1981, Gordon Lee was dismissed. He was a hard-working manager but his best was simply not good enough for a club which has always demanded success.

LELLO, CYRIL. Cyril Lello played wartime football for Lincoln City and in December 1943 scored seven goals in a League North match against Notts County. He later played for Shrewsbury Town from where he signed for Everton in September 1947. Lello made his debut in a 4–2 home win over Wolverhampton Wanderers, and scored both goals for the Blues in a 2–1 win at Middlesbrough the following week. Although he had joined Everton as an inside-forward, he was converted to wing-half. He suffered a serious injury towards the end of the 1949–50 season and missed the whole of the following campaign at the end of which the Goodison Park club were relegated. However, he was an ever-present in 1953–54 when the club regained their place in the top flight and also in 1954–55, the Blues ending their first season back in the first division in mid-table. After having played in 254 league and Cup games for Everton, Lello was signed by Rochdale manager Harry Catterick, a former team-mate. However, he was forced to retire after just 11 outings for the Spotland club.

LIMPAR, ANDERS. Anders Limpar began his career playing in Sweden for Brommapojk and Orgryte before joining Young Boys of Berne in 1988–89. He tried his luck in Italian football with Cremonese before joining Arsenal for £1 million in July 1990. Following his exciting performances for Sweden in the 1990 World Cup finals, Limpar added a new dimension to the Gunners' attack, scoring a hat-trick in the final match of the season as the Highbury club won the league championship. Although he scored some spectacular goals for Arsenal, his talents weren't always appreciated by manager George Graham and in March 1994 he joined Everton for a fee of £1.6 million. Limpar made his debut for the Blues in a 1–0 home defeat by Tottenham Hotspur. He spent much of his Goodison career in and out of the side due to injuries and competition for places, but he was inspirational in the club's 1995 FA Cup final victory over Manchester United. He went on to score six goals in 78 league and Cup games before, in January 1997, being allowed to join Birmingham City.

LINDSAY, JACK. A strong-tackling full-back with good distribution, Jack Lindsay joined the Toffees from Glasgow Rangers for a fee of £7,000 in 1951. He proved to be a useful signing but arrived too late to prevent the club from being relegated that season. He remained the club's first-choice left-back for the next three seasons until he broke a leg in the 1–1 draw at home to Stoke City on 10 April 1954. However, he had played his part that season in helping the club win promotion to the first division, scoring his only goals for the Blues in a 6–2 win at Derby County and two weeks later in an 8–4 victory over Plymouth Argyle at Goodison Park. Unable to regain his first-team place, Lindsay left the club in May 1956, moving to Bury with team-mate John Parker. But after just one season at Gigg Lane, during which he made just seven appearances, he left to end his career with South Liverpool.

LINEKER, GARY. An outstanding talent of his generation, Gary Lineker began his career with Leicester City. His 46 first division goals in his final two seasons at Filbert Street made him the hottest property in Britain. He arrived at Goodison Park in June 1985 for a fee of £800,000 – a figure set by an independent tribunal. Although he was to play for only one season for the Blues, he struck up a superb attacking partnership with Graeme Sharp and scored 30 goals in 41 league games plus another eight in Cup competitions. His league total included hat-tricks against Birmingham City (home 4–1), Manchester City (home 4–0) and Southampton (home 6–1). Despite Lineker's heroics, Everton finished runners-up to Liverpool in both the league and the FA Cup. Consolation was gained, however, from the fact that he was named the PFA Footballer of the Year and won the Golden Boot award as the top scorer in the World Cup finals with six goals. He made an important contribution to England's 1986 World Cup campaign in Mexico, a first-half Lineker hat-trick blitzing away Poland. As soon as the finals were over, he moved to Barcelona for a staggering £2.3 million. With the Spanish side he won a Spanish Cup and a European Cup-Winners' Cup medal but in June 1989 he followed Terry Venables, his manager at Barcelona, to White Hart Lane for a fee of £1.2 million. In his first season at Spurs, he scored 24 goals which meant he headed the first division scoring charts. By now he was an integral member of the

Gary Lineker

England squad which played so well to reach the semi-finals of Italia '90. In 1991, he helped Spurs win the FA Cup. Never booked in the whole of his career, Lineker's services to football were rewarded in the 1992 New Year's Honours List with the OBE. For England, he scored 48 goals in 80 appearances – just one goal away from equalling Bobby Charlton's record. He announced he would be ending his career in Japan and in February 1993 he joined Nagoya Grampus Eight for £1.7 million, attaining immediate superstar status. Lineker now has a new career as a national radio and television personality.

LITTLEWOODS CUP. See Football League Cup.

LIVERPOOL. The first league derby between Everton and Liverpool took place on 13 October 1894. The Blues won 3–0 with goals by Bell, Latta and McInnes. A month later when the teams met at Anfield, the game ended in a 2–2 draw with honours even. The two teams first met in the FA Cup in 1901–2. After holding the Reds to a 2–2 draw at

Anfield and twice being behind, Everton started the replay at Goodison as favourites. However, after Walter Balmer had put through his own net, they never really recovered and conceded another goal just before the final whistle. One of Everton's finest derby victories came in their league championship-winning season of 1914–15 when they won 5–0 at Anfield with Bobby Parker netting a hat-trick. The highlight of the 1948–49 season was the drawn derby game with Liverpool which attracted a record gate to Goodison of 78,299. In 1977, the two clubs met in the FA Cup semi-final for what was the fourth time. On previous occasions, the Reds had always triumphed and this was to prove no exception even though it required two attempts. In the first game, with the score at 2–2, Bryan Hamilton scored what appeared to be the winner, only for referee Clive Thomas to rule him offside. In 1984, the clubs met in a Wembley League Cup final – it was the game all Merseyside had dreamed of. After 90 minutes there were no goals. In extra-time and with the minutes ticking away, Adrian Heath shot and, with Grobbelaar beaten, Phil Neal raced in to clear off the line. In the replay at Maine Road a goal by Graeme Souness settled the battle in Liverpool's favour. On 10 May 1986, the clubs met at Wembley in the first-ever all-Merseyside FA Cup final. The Blues took the lead through Gary Lineker who steered the ball home for his 40th goal of the season, but two goals from Rush and one from Craig Johnston gave Liverpool the Cup. Arguably the greatest Merseyside derby of all-time was the FA Cup fifth-round replay at Goodison Park on 20 February 1991. Liverpool took the lead after 32 minutes when Peter Beardsley stabbed home a low drive but two minutes after the interval, Graeme Sharp headed Everton level. Beardsley scored a magnificent solo goal after 70 minutes but within three minutes Sharp equalised for a second time. Rush put the Reds back in front but with just 90 seconds remaining, substitute Tony Cottee equalised to take the tie into extra-time. John Barnes scored a spectacular fourth for Liverpool, bending a 25-yard shot inside Southall's post. There were just three minutes left on the clock when Cottee burst through a static Liverpool defence to make the score 4–4.

LIVINGSTONE, DUGGIE. Duggie Livingstone joined Glasgow Celtic as a youngster but being unable to break into the side on a regular basis, he moved south to join Everton. He made his debut for the Blues at full-back in a 2–1 defeat against Manchester United at Old Trafford in September 1921. A cool, calculating defender, his lack of speed let him down and after appearing in exactly 100 league and Cup games he moved to Plymouth Argyle. In and out of the side at Home

Park he returned to Scotland with Aberdeen and after 81 appearances for the Dons he moved back to the Liverpool area to play for Tranmere Rovers. Two years later he was appointed trainer at Exeter City before moving to Sheffield United in a similar capacity. In 1949, he became manager of Sparta of Rotterdam but within a couple of years he was on the move again, this time to become the Republic of Ireland team manager. He later managed Belgium and took them to the 1954 World Cup finals before being appointed manager of Newcastle United. In his first season at St James's Park, the Magpies won the FA Cup but after a furious row with the Newcastle board he left to take charge at Fulham before ending his managerial career with Chesterfield.

Mick Lyons

LYONS, MICK. Croxteth-born Mick Lyons joined the club as a striker and played in the forward role in both Youth and Central League teams. When David Johnson emerged from the shadows, Tommy Casey decided to switch Lyons to centre-back. He made his first-team debut for the Blues in a 3–2 defeat at Nottingham Forest in March 1971 and went on to build an outstanding career, playing in 460 first-team games for the club. By the mid 1970s, Lyons had won his spurs, fully deserving the England Under-23 caps, B international recognition and club captaincy that came his way. Throughout his 12 years at Goodison he never finished on the winning side in a Merseyside derby, missing the only two Everton victories. There were also moments of despair for the player who was 'Mr Everton' to many supporters – a player who would readily run through a brick wall to further the Everton cause. In 1979, after he had volleyed a 40-yard own goal past a dumbfounded George Wood at Anfield, he was approached by a joyful Everton supporter in a pub who announced that he couldn't be happier, for he'd drawn Lyons' name in a sweep as the scorer of the first goal and won £40. After losing his first-team place in 1982 he severed his long association with the club and joined Sheffield Wednesday. He helped the Owls into the first division before becoming player-coach at Grimsby Town but after the Mariners were relegated to the third division in 1986–87 he was sacked. A month later he rejoined the Goodison club as coach under Colin Harvey before taking similar jobs, first with Wigan Athletic and then Huddersfield Town. He later accepted the post of coach to the Brunei national team.

M

MACONNACHIE, JOHN. Aberdeen-born defender John Maconnachie began his career with Hibernian, playing most of his games at left-back, before signing for Everton in April 1907. He made his first-team debut for the Goodison Park club at centre-half in a 2–1 home win over Preston North End in the third match of the 1907–8 season. As the season unfolded, the unflappable Scot began to establish himself in his more customary left-back role and in 1908–9 was an important member of the Everton side that finished runners-up in the first division. One of the most skilful defenders ever to represent the club, Maconnachie scored only seven goals in 270 league and Cup appearances with three of them coming in the first four games of the 1912–13 season, including two in a 4–1 win at Derby County. After appearing in wartime games for the club, he continued to turn out for the first team in 1919–20 but at the end of that season he left Goodison to join Swindon Town.

MAKEPEACE, HARRY. Harry Makepeace represented England at both football and cricket, a distinction he shared with his Everton and Lancashire team-mate Jack Sharp. Born in Middlesbrough, he moved to Liverpool at the age of ten, giving Everton the chance to sign him from Bootle Amateurs in the summer of 1902. He made his debut for the Goodison Park club the following February in a 3–1 fourth round FA Cup win over Manchester United. Makepeace had begun his career as an inside-forward but in 1904–5 was switched to wing-half with great success. A regular member of the Everton side from 1904 to 1914, he played in the FA Cup-winning team of 1906 and again in the

1907 final. He was capped four times by England, against Scotland in 1906, 1910 and 1912, and against Wales in 1912. He also represented the Football League in 1910. Although the First World War effectively ended his playing career, Harry Makepeace, who scored 23 goals in 336 league and Cup games, returned to renew his long-running Goodison connection by becoming the club's coach after a spell working in Holland. His cricketing career continued to flourish and he opened for England on four occasions, scoring a century against Australia in Melbourne in the 1920–21 tour.

MANAGERS. Below is a complete list of Everton's full-time managers with the inclusive dates during which they held office.

Theo Kelly	1939–1948	Howard Kendall	1981–1987
Cliff Britton	1948–1956	Colin Harvey	1987–1990
Ian Buchan	1956–1958	Howard Kendall	1990–1993
Johnny Carey	1958–1961	Mike Walker	1994
Harry Catterick	1961–1973	Joe Royle	1994–1997
Billy Bingham	1973–1977	Howard Kendall	1997–1998
Gordon Lee	1977–1981	Walter Smith	1998–

MARATHON MATCHES. Everton have been involved in two FA Cup games that have gone to four matches. The first was in 1887–88 when the club were drawn to play away at Bolton Wanderers. After losing the first game 1–0, Everton raised a successful objection to the eligibility of Bolton player Struthers. There followed two drawn matches before Everton won the fourth meeting 2–1. Bolton claimed that seven Everton 'amateurs' had been offered money to play. The Blues lost 6–0 to Preston North End in the next round before they were informed that the FA had eliminated them anyway. Bolton then met North End in a rearranged match and lost 9–0. The 'Everton seven' were declared professionals and the whole club suspended for a month. One hundred years later, the club were involved in their second four-match marathon. Drawn against Sheffield Wednesday in the third round of the FA Cup, the first three meetings all ended 1–1 before the Blues travelled to Hillsborough on a wet and windy night for the fourth meeting between the clubs. In a game totally dominated by the Goodison club, Graeme Sharp netted a hat-trick in a 5–0 win.

MARKSMEN – LEAGUE. Everton's top league goalscorer is Dixie Dean who struck 349 league goals during his 14 years at Goodison Park. Only six players have hit more than 100 league goals for the club.

1.	Dixie Dean	349
2.	Graeme Sharp	111
3.	Alex Young	110
4.	Bob Latchford	106
5.	Joe Royle	102
6.	Roy Vernon	101
7.	Edgar Chadwick	97
8.	Dave Hickson	95
9.	Alf Milward	85
10.	John Willie Parker	82
	Alex Stevenson	82

MARKSMEN – OVERALL. Eight players have hit a century of goals for Everton. The club's top marksman is Dixie Dean. The Century Club consists of:

1.	Dixie Dean	377
2.	Graeme Sharp	146
3.	Bob Latchford	135
4.	Alex Young	125
5.	Joe Royle	115
6.	Dave Hickson	111
7.	Edgar Chadwick	110
8.	Roy Vernon	109

MARTIN, GEORGE. A man of many talents, George Martin was a gifted sculptor and a fine singer, making a number of records during the early 1940s. He was also an inside-forward of considerable ability and after first playing in the Football League with Hull City, he joined Everton in March 1928. Martin made his debut in a 1–0 defeat at Leicester City but then scored three goals in the remaining games of that campaign as Dixie Dean completed his historic 60 goals in the club's league championship-winning season. He went on to score 32 goals in 86 games before leaving to join Middlesbrough. The Lanarkshire-born forward moved to Luton Town in 1933 and spent the rest of his playing days with the Kenilworth Road club. After the Second World War, he was made manager of the Hatters before taking charge at Newcastle United, leading the Magpies to promotion from the second division. He later managed Aston Villa but had difficult relationships with the board and left in controversial circumstances when he was forced to resign. He rejoined Luton Town but his second spell proved to be an unhappy experience as the club went down to the fourth division.

McBAIN, NEIL. Neil McBain was manager of New Brighton when he found himself a player short – a goalkeeper – for a third division (North) match at Hartlepool United in March 1947. Deciding to wear the goalkeeper's jersey himself, at the age of 52 years 4 months he became the oldest player to appear in a Football League match. For the record, New Brighton lost 3–0. He started his playing career with Manchester United, making 43 first-team appearances before signing for Everton in early 1923. His transfer led to more than a thousand United supporters packing into a local hall to protest about his departure. An elegant wing-half, he made his debut for the Goodison Park club in a 3–1 home win over Chelsea on 10 February 1923. He went on to play in 103 first-team games, his only goal coming in a 4–1 defeat at Arsenal in October 1925. After one more match he left Everton to play for Liverpool, followed by spells with St Johnstone and Watford. He was capped three times by Scotland during his Everton career. McBain entered management with Watford and spent some time in charge of New Brighton, Luton Town and Leyton Orient. Disappointed with the English game, he went to South America to coach the Argentinian side Estudiantes de la Plata.

McDONALD, JOHN. Signed from Airdrie in the summer of 1920, the hard-tackling full-back made his debut in a 3–3 draw at Bradford Park Avenue on the opening day of the 1920–21 season. A year later he was appointed the club's captain and was the inspiration behind Everton's successful struggle to avoid relegation. McDonald, who had won Scottish representative honours during the First World War, was unlucky not to win full international honours during his seven seasons at Goodison Park. He turned in many good performances, but the club were always struggling in the lower reaches of the first division. He played in 224 league and Cup games for the Blues before moving on, ending his career with New Brighton in August 1927.

McKENZIE, DUNCAN. Beginning his career with Nottingham Forest, Duncan McKenzie made his league debut for the City Ground club at Sunderland in September 1969; it was the only game in which he played that season. When he was given another chance at first-team level, he could not produce the form he had been showing for the reserves and was loaned out to Mansfield Town. Seven goals in his first six games for the Stags persuaded the Forest management to give him another chance. The Grimsby-born forward responded magnificently to top the second division scoring charts in 1973–74

Duncan McKenzie

and end the season with 28 league and Cup goals in his 49 appearances. Also that season, he was on the England substitutes' bench for the Home International championships but was not called upon to play. After scoring 46 goals in 124 league and Cup games he was allowed to join Leeds United for £240,000. A turbulent time at Elland Road persuaded him to leave English football to play for Belgian side Anderlecht. Thirty games and 16 goals later, he was signed by Everton boss Billy Bingham for £200,000, and made his debut in a 4–2 defeat at Coventry City in December 1976. With Bingham losing his job just days after McKenzie's arrival, new manager Gordon Lee never saw eye to eye with the Everton player and in September 1978 he left to join Chelsea. He later played for Blackburn Rovers before playing in the NASL for Tulsa Roughnecks and Chicago Sting. McKenzie was a tremendous showman and seemed to spend more time amusing supporters by jumping over cars than actually playing football!

Steve McMahon

McMAHON, STEVE. A former Goodison ball-boy, Steve McMahon joined Everton as an apprentice in December 1977 and made his first-team debut in a 3–1 defeat at Sunderland on the opening day of the 1980–81 season. Voted Player of the Year in 1981–82 by supporters who appreciated his total commitment, he won international recognition when he was chosen to play for England Under-21s against the Republic of Ireland. Although he continued to perform at a consistently high level, the team as a whole were going through a bad spell and so, in an effort to further his career, he refused to sign a new contract when his current one expired at the end of the 1982–83 season. Manager Howard Kendall wanted him to stay but McMahon was adamant and in May 1983 he joined Aston Villa for £175,000. He played in 87 league and Cup games for Villa before, in September 1985, he became Kenny Dalglish's first major signing when he moved to Anfield for £375,000. Ironically, his first goal for the Reds was the winner at Goodison as the Anfield side went on to win the league championship in his first season with the club. In February 1988 he won the first of 17 full international caps for England when he played against Israel in Tel Aviv. He went on to win three league championship medals and two FA Cup medals with Liverpool but, after appearing in 261 league and Cup games, he left Anfield in December 1991 to join Manchester City. Three years later he became player-manager of Swindon Town and in his first season inspired the Wiltshire club to the second division championship after the club had suffered two successive relegations.

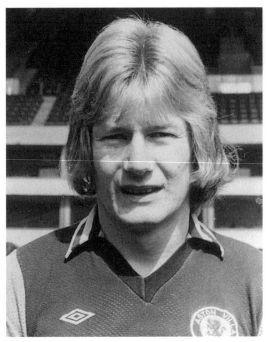

Ken McNaught

McNAUGHT, KEN. A tough, rugged Scot, Ken McNaught joined Everton straight from school and made his first-team debut in a 3–0 home win over Leicester City in January 1975. In 1976–77, he was Everton's only ever-present, appearing in all the club's 58 league and Cup games and scoring his only three goals for the club. After appearing in 86 games for the Goodison Park club, he was allowed to leave and joined Aston Villa for £200,000. He soon established himself alongside Welsh international Leighton Phillips in the heart of the Villa defence, but he was partnered by Allan Evans when the club won the league championship in 1980–81. In the following campaign, he won a European Cup winners' medal. He played in 259 first-team games for Villa before moving to nearby West Bromwich Albion. After playing in every league and Cup game for the Hawthorns club in

1983–84, he went on loan to Manchester City before signing for Sheffield United. A year later he was forced to retire through injury and in 1988 he was appointed coach to Dunfermline.

MEAGAN, MICK. A versatile performer, Mick Meagan began his career with Republic of Ireland junior clubs, Rathfarnham and Johnville, before signing for Everton in September 1952. He turned professional some 18 months later, but he had to wait until the opening game of the 1957–58 season to make his debut in a 1–0 home win over Wolverhampton Wanderers. That season Meagan scored his only goal for the club in a 3–1 win over Sunderland at Goodison Park. The Dublin-born player went on to make 175 first-team appearances for Everton before, in the summer of 1964, he joined Huddersfield Town, Ray Wilson coming in the opposite direction with a cash adjustment. Having won his first international cap for the Republic of Ireland against Scotland in 1961, Meagan continued to represent his country and was made captain of Huddersfield. He appeared in 119 league games for the Terriers before joining Halifax Town in July 1968.

MERCER, JOE. One of the game's all-time greats, Joe Mercer had a wonderful career both as a player and a manager. He began as a junior with Everton in 1932 and stayed with them until 1946. During that time he developed into one of the finest wing-halves in the country and helped the Goodison Park club to the league championship in 1938–39. He lost seven seasons of top-class soccer but played regularly in wartime soccer, being part of a famous England half-back line with Stan Cullis and Cliff Britton. Out of favour with Everton, he moved to Arsenal where his career was rejuvenated. He captained the Gunners to the league championship in 1947–48 and played in his first FA Cup final for the club in 1950 when they beat Liverpool. Mercer was voted Footballer of the Year in 1950 and gained another league championship medal in 1952–53. His illustrious playing career came to an end when he broke his leg in April 1954 against Blackpool at Highbury just before his 40th birthday. Mercer went into management, first with Sheffield United and then with Aston Villa. At Villa Park, he saw the club promoted from the second division, reach two FA Cup semi-finals and win the League Cup. However, in 1964, Mercer suffered a stroke due to over-work. The Villa directors waited until he was over the worst effects, then sacked him! Most people thought his retirement was permanent but in the summer of 1965 he made a comeback as manager of Manchester City. He revitalised a club that had been in the doldrums, winning the second division title in 1965–66, then the league championship two years later.

More trophies followed as City beat Leicester to take the 1969 FA Cup final and the European Cup-Winners' Cup the following year. In 1972, he moved to become general manager at Coventry City and in 1974 took temporary charge of the England team. Awarded the OBE for his services to football, one of Everton's most beloved sons died on his 76th birthday at his Merseyside home.

MILK CUP. See Football League Cup.

MILWARD, ALF. Born at Great Marlow, Alf Milward joined Everton from Old Borlasians and Marlow in 1888 and quickly established himself as a first-team regular. He made his debut in a 3–0 defeat at Blackburn Rovers in the club's first season in the Football League. Along with Edgar Chadwick he formed a left-wing partnership for Everton that was second to none, both of them scoring goals with regularity. He performed with great consistency for the club between 1888 and 1897 and was rewarded with four full international caps for England. At Goodison, Milward won two FA Cup winners' medals and a league championship medal. He scored two hat-tricks for the club – against Derby County in an 11–2 FA Cup victory in 1889–90 and a 3–0 league win at Small Heath in 1895–96. In 1897, after scoring 96 goals in 224 league and Cup games, he left Everton to join New Brighton Tower. Two years later he signed for Southampton and in two seasons at The Dell never missed a Southern League game. In his first season, he was the club's top scorer and helped them reach the FA Cup final, scoring two of the goals that helped defeat Millwall 3–0 in the semi-final replay. The following season he was joined by Edgar Chadwick and the former Everton stars helped the Saints win the Southern League championship. In the close season of 1901, he signed for New Brompton before retiring two years later.

MOONLIGHT DRIBBLERS. This was the nickname given to Everton by some humorists early on in their history. The nickname reflected the reputation the team had for training after dark, relying largely upon the light of the moon to illuminate their efforts.

MOORE, ERIC. Haydock-born Eric Moore played at both wing-half and centre-forward in the club's Central League side but was converted into a full-back after signing professional forms. He made his first-team debut in a 3–1 home win over Middlesbrough in December 1949 and for the next year and a half was a regular in the Everton side. A knee injury sidelined him for long spells during the next couple of seasons and it was 1954–55 before he re-established himself in the side. Having missed just one game that season, he was an ever-present in 1955–56 but, after making just one first division appearance the following season, his 184th first-team game, he left the club to play for Chesterfield for a fee of £10,000. He stayed at Saltergate for six months before ending his league career with Tranmere Rovers for whom he made 36 league appearances.

MOORES, JOHN. A former amateur footballer, John Moores was a member of the family which founded the Littlewoods Football Pools and mail-order organisation. A millionaire football fanatic, he became chief benefactor of a club he had supported from childhood. However,

John Moores

progress was not fast enough for him and, in 1961, Everton manager Johnny Carey was offered a golden handshake by Moores. Harry Catterick took over at Goodison with instructions from Moores to get to the top with good football, and in the 1960s with Moores as backer and director, that is just what Catterick achieved. They won the league title and FA Cup and were regular participants in Europe. John Moores had achieved his ambition of guiding Everton Football Club back to fame and respect.

MORRISSEY, JOHNNY. Winger Johnny Morrissey arrived at Goodison from neighbours Liverpool for a fee of £10,000 in

September 1962. After making his debut in a 4–1 home win over Sheffield Wednesday, and having a hand in three of the goals, he quickly established himself as a first-team regular. He scored his first goal in the 2–2 home draw against Liverpool seven matches later. Although he didn't score that many goals himself – 50 in his 314 first-team games – he did score the all-important, dramatic penalty winner against Leeds United in the 1968 FA Cup semi-final at Old Trafford. Unfortunately, he had to be satisfied with a runners-up medal as the Blues lost 1–0 to West Bromwich Albion in the final. In 1969–70, when Everton won the league championship, Morrissey played in all but one game, creating many of Joe Royle's 23 goals. Two seasons later, though, he found his place threatened and left to play for Oldham Athletic but after just six league games for the Boundary Park club, injury forced his retirement from the game.

MOST GOALS IN A SEASON. When Everton won the second division championship in 1930–31, they scored 121 goals in 42 matches. They scored in every home game and failed to score in only two games away from Goodison Park – Tottenham Hotspur (0–1) and Stoke City (0–2). The Blues scored 76 goals at home and in 12 of the home games scored four or more goals. Plymouth Argyle were beaten 9–1, Charlton Athletic 7–1 and Oldham Athletic 6–4. The club also won 7–0 at the Valley to complete the double over luckless Charlton. The club's top scorer was Dixie Dean with 39 goals (including four in the victories over Plymouth and Oldham).

MOST MATCHES. Everton played their most matches, 63, in seasons 1984–85 and 1985–86. In 1984–85, this comprised 42 league games, seven FA Cup games, four League Cup games, nine European Cup-Winners' Cup games and an appearance in the Charity Shield. In 1985–86, the total included 42 league games, seven FA Cup games, five League Cup games, eight Screen Super Cup games and another appearance in the Charity Shield.

MOUNTFIELD, DEREK. After playing in only 30 games for fourth division Tranmere Rovers, Derek Mountfield joined Everton, the club he had supported as a schoolboy, for £30,000 in the summer of 1982. He made his league debut at Birmingham City in April 1983 and the following season was given the opportunity to press for a regular first-team spot when Mark Higgins suffered the first of a number of injuries. Within five years at Goodison, he had gained an FA Cup winners' medal, two league championship medals, a European Cup-Winners'

Cup medal and two Charity Shield medals, as well as being capped by England at both Under-21 and B level. During the club's magnificent 1984–85 season, Mountfield scored 14 league and Cup goals from the centre-half position, including the last-minute equaliser against Ipswich Town in the FA Cup quarter-final and the semi-final extra-time winner against Luton Town. Following the arrival of Dave Watson, Mountfield, who had played in 139 league and Cup games, moved to Aston Villa in June 1988 for £450,000. He was hampered by injuries during his four years at Villa Park, but nevertheless played in 120 games, scoring 17 goals before joining Wolverhampton Wanderers. In 1994 he moved to Carlisle United and was a key member of their 1994–95 championship-winning team. He later played for Northampton Town before signing for Walsall.

N

NEUTRAL GROUNDS. Goodison Park has been used as a neutral ground for FA Cup matches on a number of occasions and as early as April 1895 staged an international match when England beat Scotland 3–0. Everton's ground was chosen as the venue of the 1894 FA Cup final between Bolton Wanderers and Notts County and a crowd of 37,000 saw County run out 4–1 winners. The club was honoured again in 1910 when the FA Cup final replay between Barnsley and Newcastle United drew an audience of 69,000. FA Cup semi-finals also became a regular feature at the ground. Goodison continued to stage internationals and was the venue for England's first defeat on home soil by a non-British side, when Eire won 2–0 in September 1949 with Everton's Peter Farrell netting one of the goals. In 1966, Goodison Park was one of the grounds chosen for the World Cup finals with Brazil, Bulgaria, Hungary and Portugal all playing their group matches there. In the quarter-final, Portugal defeated North Korea 5–3 in one of the competition's most memorable games, while in one of the least noteworthy, West Germany beat the Soviet Union for a place in the final. In recent years, Goodison has staged few internationals with all England's home fixtures being played at Wembley but in 1995 it did host the Brazil v Japan match. Everton themselves have had to replay on a neutral ground a number of times, and their FA Cup semi-finals were played on neutral grounds. In the League Cup competition of 1976–77, the replayed final match was played at Hillsborough and, following another draw, a second replay was played at Old Trafford, the Blues losing 3–2 to Aston Villa. In 1983–84, the replayed final against Liverpool was played at Maine Road with the Reds winning 1–0. The

Pat Nevin

club's six appearances in the FA Charity Shield at Old Trafford and Wembley also qualify for inclusion as do the finals of the Simod Cup and Zenith Data Systems Cup, both played at Wembley. The club played numerous Cup finals at Fallowfield, Crystal Palace and Wembley and the Blues' 3–1 win over Rapid Vienna in the European Cup-Winners' Cup final was played on neutral territory in Rotterdam.

NEVIN, PAT. Glasgow-born Pat Nevin began his career with Clyde before coming south of the border to join Chelsea for £95,000 in the summer of 1983. At Stamford Bridge he won the first of 28 international caps for Scotland and scored 42 goals in 227 league and Cup games, but after five distinguished years he left the London club to sign for Everton. The two clubs were unable to agree on the size of the transfer fee and so the matter was placed before an independent tribunal which fixed the fee at £925,000. Nevin's early days at Goodison were testing, for in only his third game he damaged his knee ligaments and was sidelined for three months. Frustrated at being out of the team, he tried to come back too early, but by the end of the season he had returned and scored vital goals in two Cup semi-finals. He went on to play in 138 league and Cup games for the Blues before moving across the Mersey to play for Tranmere Rovers. The PFA Chairman has been a great ambassador for Tranmere and has played in over 200 league games for the Prenton Park club.

NEWTON, HENRY. After making 282 league appearances for Nottingham Forest, Henry Newton signed for Everton in October 1970 for £150,000 plus Northern Ireland international Tommy Jackson. He had been pursued by Derby County manager Brian Clough but turned down the Rams' persuasive boss to accept the terms offered by Harry Catterick. He made his debut for the Blues in a disastrous 4–0 defeat at Arsenal and thereafter his Goodison career was hampered by a number of long-term injuries. Despite these setbacks, he gave his best performances after he had been switched from half-back to left-back to replace his namesake Keith Newton. He went on to play in 83 league and Cup games in three years at Goodison Park before Clough finally got his man in September 1973. He won a league championship medal in 1974–75 but again struggled to overcome a series of injuries before ending his league career with Walsall.

NEWTON, KEITH. A fine attacking full-back, Keith Newton began his career with Blackburn Rovers and was a member of the team which won the FA Youth Cup in 1959. Able to play in both full-back positions, his full international debut came at left-back in a Wembley rehearsal against West Germany in February 1966. He missed out on the World Cup later that year, but went on to win 27 caps. He joined Everton for £80,000 in December 1969 and played his part in bringing the league championship to Goodison in his first season, although he missed the run-in with injury. That summer he was off to Mexico with England's World Cup squad, playing his last international in the epic quarter-final defeat by West Germany in Leon. Back at Goodison, Keith Newton was unable to sustain his previous high level of performance and for the next two seasons was in and out of the Everton side. There were reports of a rift with manager Harry Catterick who failed to appreciate that Newton liked to play his way out of tight corners and in May 1972 he was given a free transfer. He joined Burnley and in his first season at Turf Moor was one of six ever-presents as the Clarets swept to the second division title. He missed very few matches in his Burnley career, playing the last of 253 first-team games at Brighton in February 1978 at the age of 36. He later played non-league football for Morecambe and Clitheroe.

NICKNAMES. Near Goodison Park was Mother Noblett's Toffee Shop, which might have helped Everton get the nickname 'The Toffees' or 'The Toffeemen'. Near the Queen's Head Hotel where Everton was first named was Ye Anciente Everton Toffee House, so there are at least two claimants to the honour. Many players in the club's history have been fondly known by their nicknames including:

1888–1898	Johnny Holt – Little Everton Devil
1934–1947	Dicky Downs – Stonewall
1958–1962	Bobby Collins – The Little General
1960–1968	Alex Young – The Golden Vision
1963–1967	Alex Scott – Chico
1964–1973	Jimmy Husband – Skippy
1992–1996	Gary Ablett – Ninja

NON-LEAGUE. Everton have a very good record against non-league clubs in the FA Cup competition, though they were defeated on one occasion. That was on 27 January 1900 when former Everton player Alf Milward scored two goals against the Blues in a 3–0 win for Southern League Southampton at The Dell. The Saints went on to reach the final that year but lost 4–0 to Bury at Crystal Palace. The club's full record against non-league opposition in the FA Cup is as follows:

Date	Opposition	Venue	Score
28.01.1899	Jarrow	Home	3–1
27.01.1900	Southampton	Away	0–3
09.02.01	Southampton	Away	3–1
13.01.12	Clapton Orient	Away	2–1
08.01.27	Poole Town	Home	3–1
06.01.62	King's Lynn	Home	4–0
12.02.66	Bedford Town	Away	3–0
04.01.75	Altrincham	Home	1–1
07.01.75	Altrincham	Away	2–0 *
16.02.85	Telford United	Home	3–0
27.01.91	Woking	Home	1–0

*Played at Old Trafford

NULTY, GEOFF. A boyhood Liverpool fan, Geoff Nulty's versatility was in evidence during his schooldays when he played at both centre-half and centre-forward. At his first club, Stoke City, he played mainly at left-back but appeared occasionally in goal! Failing to break into the first team at the Victoria Ground, he joined Burnley on a free transfer and scored on his full debut for the Clarets in a League Cup win at Rotherham United. He also scored on his full league debut against Manchester United. After helping the Turf Moor club win the second division championship in 1972–73 he was transferred to Newcastle United for £130,000. He immediately secured a first-team place and was appointed club captain the following summer. However, following the Magpies' relegation in 1978 he moved to Everton for £40,000, rejoining former Newcastle boss Gordon Lee. A polished defender, Nulty's career was brought to an abrupt end after just 38 appearances in an Everton shirt following a tackle by Liverpool's Jimmy Case in the derby game at Goodison Park in March 1980. Strong in the tackle, he made the first of those appearances in a 1–0 win at Chelsea on the opening day of the 1978–79 season. Three days later he scored the winning goal in a 2–1 win over Derby County at Goodison Park. Although he had prepared for life after football by taking an Open University degree in social sciences, he took a coaching job at Everton under Gordon Lee, later following him to Preston North End.

NUMBERING. In 1932–33 Everton were the first football team to wear the numbers 1–11 when they stepped out for their 3–0 FA Cup final victory over Manchester City, who wore numbers 12–22.

O

OLDEST PLAYER. The oldest player to line up in an Everton first team is Ted Sagar. He played the last of his 495 league and Cup games against Plymouth Argyle (away 0–1) on 15 November 1952 at the age of 42 years 281 days.

O'NEILL, JIMMY. Dublin-born goalkeeper Jimmy O'Neill made his league debut for Everton in a 4–0 defeat at Middlesbrough on 23 August 1950. Signed from Bulfin United, he went on to have 11 great years at Goodison and was an integral part of the Everton scene. One of the country's outstanding goalkeepers, he won the first of 17 full caps for the Republic of Ireland against Spain in 1952. In 1953–54, he helped Everton win promotion to the first division and the following season produced some memorable performances as the Blues consolidated their position in the top flight. A goalkeeper of the highest authority on his day, he played in 213 games for Everton before joining Stoke City for £2,000 in July 1960. At the Victoria Ground he was an ever-present in 1962–63 as the Potters won the second division championship. He later played for Darlington and Port Vale before leaving the game.

OVERSEAS PLAYERS. Stefan Rehn joined Everton from Djurgardens IF in June 1989 and made his debut in the 1–0 win at Charlton Athletic on 16 September that year. Ray Atteveld was signed from RJC Haarlem in August 1989 and went on to play in 63 games for the Blues before joining Bristol City in March 1992. Robert Warzycha signed for the Blues in March 1991 from Polish club Gornik Zabrze and went on to appear in 110 league and Cup games. Belgrade-born Radosavijevic, better known as Preki, made 47 league appearances before joining Portsmouth. Anders Limpar, the Swedish international winger, was signed by Mike Walker from Arsenal in March 1994. Just before the Everton manager lost his job, he splashed out £3 million on Daniel Amokachi, the highly rated Nigerian World Cup star. Russian international winger Andrei Kanchelskis signed for Everton for £5 million after a well-publicised bust up with Manchester United manager Alex Ferguson and protracted negotiations. Swiss international Marc Hottiger joined Everton from Newcastle United for £700,000 in March 1996 in a transfer long delayed by a work-permit dispute. Danish international Claus Thomsen, who played in Euro '96, joined the Blues from Ipswich Town. The last overseas player to sign for the club was Croatian international Slaven Bilic who joined the Blues from West Ham United for £4.5 million in May 1997. Some Everton players, though not born on foreign shores, had foreign-sounding names, notably Sam Chedgzoy and Imre Varadi.

OWN GOALS. There have been a number of instances of own goals over the years, but there are three Everton players whose misdemeanours stand out. Gordon Dugdale, who looked a certainty for England's 1950 World Cup team when he had to give up the game because of a heart complaint, once incurred the wrath of legendary Everton keeper Ted Sagar. Playing against Middlesbrough, he tried to chip the ball back but only succeeded in lifting the ball over Sagar's head for an own goal. England full-back Tommy Wright scored one of the fastest league own goals in history after just 35 seconds of the Merseyside derby in March 1972. A week later he went one better when he put through his own net after just 32 seconds of the match against Manchester City. Sandy Brown scored an own goal with a searing header from a Liverpool corner. It would have been acknowledged as brilliant if it had gone in at the right end!

P

PARKER, ALEX. Born in Irvine in Ayrshire, Alex Parker began his career as a centre-forward but was switched to wing-half shortly after joining Kelso Rovers. After moving to Falkirk, he began to play full-back and in May 1955 he won the first of 15 Scottish caps when selected against Portugal. A strong-tackling defender, he joined Everton in the summer of 1958 but was immediately posted to Cyprus with the Royal Scots Fusiliers. He didn't make his first-team debut until 8 November 1958 in a 4–2 win at Aston Villa. His first goal for the club came in the return match at Goodison later that season, giving the Blues a 2–1 win over the Villa Park club. Virtually an ever-present for the next five seasons, he went on to appear in 219 league and Cup games before leaving Goodison to finish his playing career with Southport. He later became player-manager of Irish league side Ballymena United before returning to Haig Avenue in 1970 as manager of Southport.

PARKER, BOBBY. Bobby Parker joined Everton from Glasgow Rangers in November 1913 and immediately helped solve the club's goalscoring problems. He made a goalscoring debut in a 1–1 home draw against Sheffield Wednesday and ended the season as the club's top scorer with 17 league goals in 24 games, including a hat-trick in a 5–0 Boxing Day win over Manchester United. The following season he did even better, equalling Bertie Freeman's Everton record of six years earlier, in scoring 36 league goals in 35 games. He was the first division's leading scorer and his total included hat-tricks in the wins over Liverpool (away 5–0), Sunderland (home 7–1), Manchester City (home 4–1), Aston Villa (away 5–1), Bolton Wanderers (home 5–3) and all four goals against Sheffield

Wednesday (away 4–1). Not surprisingly, Everton won the league championship that season. He continued to play for the Blues after the First World War but in May 1921, after he had scored 71 goals in 92 league and Cup games, he left Everton to join Nottingham Forest.

PARKER, JOHN WILLIE. Arriving at Goodison Park as an amateur in 1947 from St Lawrence CYMS, John Willie Parker graduated through the club's junior sides before becoming a regular member of the Central League side. He had to wait until March 1951 to make his first-team debut in a 2–0 home defeat by Blackpool. The following season he was the club's top scorer with 15 league goals in 36 games, including a hat-trick in a 5–0 home win over Hull City. In 1953–54, he again top scored with 31 goals in 38 games as the Blues finished the season runners-up in the second division, thus winning promotion to the top flight. He scored hat-tricks against Oldham Athletic (home 3–1) and Rotherham United (home 3–0) and four goals in an 8–4 home win over Plymouth Argyle. Back in the first division, Parker was again the club's top goalscorer with 19 goals in 34 league games. In total, he played 176 league and Cup games for Everton and scored 89 goals. He played his last game for them in March 1956, joining Bury a couple of months later.

PARRY, CHARLIE. Signed from Welsh junior football, Charlie Parry made his Everton debut on the opening day of the 1889–90 season, scoring in a 3–2 home win over Blackburn Rovers. He played a number of games at wing-half, but lost his place early in the 1891–92 season, returning only after he had been converted to left-back. He had made his Welsh international debut as a wing-half against England in 1891 but won his other six caps whilst with Everton at full-back. He went on to appear in 94 league and Cup games before leaving the Goodison club to join Ardwick in 1895, adding another seven Welsh international caps to his collection.

PEACOCK, JOE. Joe Peacock was a versatile player who joined the Blues from Atherton Collieries in the summer of 1919. After making his debut at right-half in a 1–0 defeat at Sheffield Wednesday in January 1920, he was switched to centre-forward for his second match. He scored the third goal in a 3–0 win over the other Sheffield club, United. He also played a number of games at inside-forward but it was as a wing-half that he made his name. He scored 12 goals in 161 games for Everton before being transferred to Middlesbrough in 1927. With the then Ayresome Park club, he won a second division championship medal in 1928–29 and was capped by England three times during their continental tour at the end of that season. He later played for Sheffield Wednesday and Clapton Orient before coaching in Sweden. In 1939, he returned to these shores to become Wrexham's trainer.

PEARSON, JIM. A Scottish Schoolboy and Youth international, Jim Pearson began his career with St Johnstone. In 1973–74, he played for the Under-23 side against Wales and was substitute for the Scottish League in the match against the Football League. At the end of that season he left St Johnstone, for whom he had scored 39 goals in 96 league games, and joined Everton for a fee of £100,000. He made his debut in a 1–1 draw at Coventry City on 21 September 1974 and scored his first goal for the club three days later in a 2–2 draw at Queens Park Rangers. He was a highly talented forward, but unfortunately he allowed his fiery temperament to disrupt his form. Bought primarily to score goals, he fell out of favour when they dried up despite an extended run in the side. So in August 1978, after scoring just 19 goals in 116 outings, he was allowed to join Newcastle United for £70,000. Pearson made an immediate impact at St James's Park, scoring three goals in his first few games before a serious injury ended his career.

PEJIC, MIKE. Starting his league career with Stoke City, Mike Pejic possessed one of the game's fiercest tackles. He won four England caps in his time at the Victoria Ground and appeared in 274 league games for the Potters before moving to Everton for a fee of £150,000 in February 1977. Pejic was seen as the last piece in manager Gordon Lee's jigsaw as the Blues tried to avoid the drop into the second division. He made his debut in a 1–0 win against his former club in the Potteries and, in the 17 games he played that season, the Blues lost only two and finished the season in ninth place. The following season he was a virtual ever-present as Everton finished third in the first division but in December 1978, during the match against Leeds United, he broke down and never played for the Goodison club again, despite eventually regaining full fitness. In September 1979, he moved to Aston Villa but after just ten games a persistent groin injury forced him to quit. After trying his hand at farming, he returned to the game as coach and manager of Northwich Victoria, Leek Town and Port Vale. Never afraid to put across his point of view, he later managed Chester City, but his stay at the Deva Stadium was short-lived and after seven months in charge he left the struggling second division club.

PENALTIES. Thomas Clinton missed a vital penalty for Everton in the FA Cup semi-final of 1953 against Bolton Wanderers at Maine Road.

Fighting back from four goals down, the Blues lost 4–3. The first-ever penalty shoot-out seen at Goodison was on 4 November 1970 when Everton played Borussia Moenchengladbach. The first leg in Germany had ended 1–1 as did the return, even after extra-time. Joe Royle began by missing and it was left to Andy Rankin to save the club from an early exit. With the score at 4–3 in Everton's favour, he flung himself full length to save magnificently from Muller. Joe Harper, signed from Aberdeen, missed a penalty on his league debut at home to Tottenham Hotspur on 16 December 1972. Fortunately, it didn't matter too much, as Everton won 3–1.

PICKERING, FRED. One of Everton's finest post-war strikers, Fred Pickering began his career as a full-back with Blackburn Rovers, but with the Ewood Park club well served in that department, his opportunities were limited. He had enjoyed success in the Rovers junior teams, helping to win the FA Youth Cup in 1959, but when he was given a chance in the first team, he failed to make a lasting impression. Rovers manager Jack Marshall decided to gamble with him at centre-forward after some powerful displays in that position with the reserves. Pickering had the happy knack of putting the ball in the net and after adding power and pace to his game, began to create a name for himself. In fact, he became so prolific, scoring 59 goals in 123 league games for Rovers, that when Harry Catterick's £85,000 bid was accepted, there was outrage in Blackburn. Arriving at Goodison in March 1964, he signalled his arrival with a hat-trick on his debut in a 6–1 defeat of Nottingham Forest. Two months later, he scored another hat-trick in his first match for England as the USA were beaten 10–0 in New York. Pickering enjoyed his best season in 1964–65 when he scored 37 goals in 51 league and Cup games, including a hat-trick in a 4–1 home win over Tottenham Hotspur. He remained in splendid form the following season and underlined his effectiveness with a scorching volley in the FA Cup quarter-final defeat of Manchester City. But Pickering was suffering with a cartilage problem which forced him to miss the semi-final victory over Manchester United. He declared himself fit for Wembley but Harry Catterick had his doubts about Pickering's ability to last 90 minutes and did not select him for the final against Sheffield Wednesday. His days seemed to be numbered and after scoring 68 goals in 107 outings for the Blues, he was allowed to join Birmingham City for £50,000. He returned to the north-west to play for Blackpool in 1969 but after helping the Seasiders win promotion, he returned to Ewood Park. Rovers boss, Ken Furphy, released him, claiming he was out of condition.

Fred Pickering

PITCH. The Goodison Park pitch measures 112 yards x 78 yards.

PLASTIC. Four Football League clubs have replaced their grass playing pitches with artificial surfaces at one stage or another. Queens Park Rangers were the first in 1981 but the Loftus Road plastic was discarded in 1988 in favour of a return to turf. Luton Town (1985), Oldham Athletic (1986) and Preston North End (1986) are the other three clubs. The Blues never played on the Deepdale plastic. They visited Loftus Road on five occasions while they had the artificial surface and scored just one goal, courtesy of Graeme Sharp, 3 January 1987. That was Everton's only success in a total of 16 league and Cup matches played on artificial surfaces.

POINTS. Under the three points for a win system which was introduced in 1981–82, Everton's best points tally is the 90 points gained in 1984–85 when the club won the first division championship. The club's best points haul under the old two points for a win system is 66 achieved in 1969–70; under the present rule, that would mean 95 points. Everton's lowest points record in the Football League occurred in 1888–89 when only 20 points were secured. The lowest in a 42-match programme is 32 in season 1950–51 when the club were relegated to the second division. The lowest number of goals scored by the club also occurred in the inaugural season of 1888–89 when Everton netted 35 times. However, that was a 22-match season and in 1971–72 when the club finished 15th in the first division, only 37 goals were scored.

POP SONGS. Everton Football Club's 'Here We Go' reached Number 14 in the charts after being released in May 1985. It was in the charts for five weeks.

POWER, PAUL. Discovered by Harry Godwin, Paul Power was a student at Leeds Polytechnic when he turned out for Manchester City reserves in the Central League. He made his league debut in August 1975 at Villa Park and, though never a prolific scorer from midfield, he opened his account with the winner in a thrilling match against Derby County which City won 4–3. In October 1979, Malcolm Allison handed Power the club captaincy and two years later his consistent performances led to him winning his only representative honours with an appearance in the England v Spain B international. In 1981, he scored from a free-kick in the FA Cup semi-final defeat of Ipswich Town but couldn't repeat the feat in the Wembley final against Tottenham Hotspur. Power's second appearance at the Twin Towers with City came in the 1986 Full Members' Cup final when Chelsea beat the Maine Road side 5–4. He had scored 36 goals in 445 first-team games for City when Howard Kendall took him away from Maine Road and gave him a place in Everton's league championship winning side. Everton were suffering a crippling injury crisis, and Power was given his debut in the 2–0 home win over Nottingham Forest on the opening day of the season. He went on to play in all but the last two matches of the club's successful campaign. Power later moved on to the coaching staff at Goodison Park but lost his job in November 1990 when Howard Kendall returned to the club. He joined the PFA as a community officer and is now their coaching secretary.

PREMIER LEAGUE. During the first season of the Premier League, 1992–93, Everton struggled to find any consistency and finished a very disappointing campaign in 13th spot. In the following season, they started brightly but by the end of the campaign were only nine minutes away from relegation. With just one game left, the club were third from bottom and desperately needed a win. After going two goals down at home to Wimbledon, the Blues fought back to win 3–2 with Graham Stuart hitting an 81st-minute winner. In 1994–95, Everton started disastrously, collecting only three points from their first 11 games. Appointing Joe Royle as manager, the club beat Liverpool 2–0 and went on to establish a club record of five games without conceding a goal. The results to the end of the season were mixed, but the Blues finished 15th with Royle having pulled off a minor miracle. In the following campaign, Everton attained their highest league position for six years and their best points total for eight years to finish sixth with 61 points. In 1996–97, the Blues' 7–1 win over Southampton was their biggest ever in the Premier League but six consecutive defeats midway through the season reduced the club to 15th place by the end of the campaign. Such was their dramatic slump, there was always the possibility of the club slipping into the bottom three. In 1997–98, Everton just avoided the drop into the first division. Drawing their last game of the season at home to Coventry City, the Blues ended the season with the same number of points as Bolton Wanderers but stayed in the Premiership on goal difference.

PROMOTION. Everton have been promoted on two occasions, both times from the second division to the first. Following the club's relegation in 1929–30, they returned to the top flight at the first attempt and in majestic style. The Blues scored 121 goals – only one short of the all-time second division record – and won the championship by a seven-point margin over runners-up Tottenham Hotspur. Top scorer was Dixie Dean with 39 goals. The last time Everton won promotion was in 1953–54 but it was an altogether closer chase. In the end, the Blues lost the divisional championship on goal average to Leicester City but edged one point ahead of Blackburn Rovers to take the runners-up spot.

Q

QUICKEST GOALS. The club's records from 1879 do not include precise goal times and so it is impossible to state accurately the club's quickest goalscorer. Dixie Dean, who scored 377 league and Cup goals in his Everton career, netted one within the opening half-minute of the FA Cup third-round tie against Liverpool on 9 January 1932. When Liverpool centre-half Bradshaw hesitated, Dean seized on the opportunity to shoot his side ahead. Liverpool, however, came back to win 2–1. The Blues did get an even quicker goal in a Merseyside derby match on 22 September 1962. Jim Furnell, the Liverpool keeper, dropped the ball as he tried to bounce it and Welsh international Roy Vernon was on hand to tap it into an empty net. Much to the Goodison crowd's amazement, the referee disallowed what would have the quickest goal – it was only a matter of seconds after the kick-off – for an apparent infringement!

R

RAITT, DAVID. Born at Buckhaven, Fife, full-back David Raitt began his career with Dundee and made a good number of Scottish League appearances for the Dens Park club before signing for Everton in May 1922. He made his debut in a 2–0 defeat at Tottenham Hotspur on 4 September 1922, soon establishing himself in the Goodison Park club's defence. Although of slight build, Raitt was strong in the tackle and had good positional sense. In his first season with the club, he was instrumental in the Toffees finishing the campaign in fifth place. He continued to be an important member of the first-team squad, although his appearances were restricted by the form of Warney Cresswell, who was obviously a first division star of the future. Raitt played in just six games in Everton's league championship-winning season of 1927–28 and before the start of the following season he had signed for Blackburn Rovers.

RANKIN, ANDY. Bootle-born goalkeeper Andy Rankin was on the verge of giving the game up and joining the police force when Harry Catterick took over as manager at Goodison Park. Rankin was persuaded to continue his career, and was rewarded in November 1963, making his first-team debut in a 2–2 draw at Nottingham Forest when regular keeper Gordon West was dropped. Although he was a talented goalkeeper, he was never able to gain a regular place in the Everton side. Many of his extended runs ended due to injury and in ten years at Goodison he made only 104 league and Cup appearances. Rankin is best remembered for his performance against Borussia Moenchengladbach in the European Cup of 1970–71. The second-round tie went into a penalty shoot-out and when Rankin brilliantly saved Muller's penalty, which was struck hard to the keeper's right, he became the hero of the hour. In November 1971, he joined Watford for £20,000 and went on to make over 300 first-team appearances for the Vicarage Road club before ending his league career with Huddersfield Town.

RAPID SCORING. All five Everton forwards – Ted Critchley, Jimmy Dunn, Dixie Dean, Tom Johnson and Jimmy Stein – scored in a 17-minute spell at the Valley against Charlton Athletic. It was a second division match on 7 February 1931. The Blues won 7–0 with Dixie Dean later completing a hat-trick.

RATCLIFFE, KEVIN. The most successful captain in Everton's history, centre-forward Kevin Ratcliffe played in the same Flintshire Schools side as Ian Rush. A number of top clubs offered Ratcliffe apprentice forms, but only one club interested him and that was Everton. When he was not kicking a ball about, he could be found on the Goodison terraces cheering on the likes of Ball and Royle. He made his debut in a goalless draw at Old Trafford, subduing the fearsome Joe Jordan, in March 1980 but spent the next two seasons in and out of the side. When he did play, most of his games were at left-back. Ratcliffe was upset by such apparent lack of recognition and by being played out of position, so he went to confront new manager Howard Kendall. At one stage there was even talk of a move to Ipswich Town when Bobby Robson showed an interest. In December 1982, his fortunes took a decisive upturn when he replaced the overweight Billy Wright alongside Mark Higgins in the heart of the Everton defence. Within 12 months he had succeeded the injury-ravaged Higgins as captain and the following March he was leading his country. In March 1984, at the age of 23, he became the youngest man since Bobby Moore some 20 years earlier to receive the FA Cup. Within the next year, he had led his team forward to pick up the FA Charity Shield, the league championship and the European Cup-Winners' Cup. Thereafter he skippered them to the runners-up spot in both the league and the FA Cup in 1985–86, and to another league title in 1986–87. Ratcliffe could read the game with instinctive shrewdness and could close down opponents instantly in moments of danger, often averting crises by clever positional play. Despite losing some of his astonishing speed, he continued to retain the style and consistency that made him one of the world's classiest central defenders. During the 1990–91 season, he lost his place to the fast-emerging Martin Keown and in January 1992 he was placed on the transfer list. In the spring of 1992, after playing in 461 league and Cup

Kevin Ratcliffe

games for the Blues, he joined Cardiff City and helped them win promotion to the new second division. Now manager of Chester City, Kevin Ratcliffe is one of Goodison Park's most revered sons.

RECEIPTS. The club's record receipts are £450,000 for the Premier League game against Liverpool on 16 April 1996. A crowd of 40,120 watched the game which ended 1–1 with Andrei Kanchelskis netting for the Blues.

REID, PETER. Peter Reid was a member of the successful Huyton Boys side that caused something of an upset when they won the English Schools Trophy in 1970. Many scouts watched the games and Reid had chances to join a number of clubs as an apprentice. He opted for Bolton Wanderers and in October 1974 made his first-team debut as a substitute in a home match against Orient. He soon established himself in the Wanderers side and was ever-present for the next two seasons. Reid's cultured midfield play and his intense desire to be involved at all times were features of Bolton's second division championship-winning

Peter Reid

side of 1977–78. That season, he also appeared in England's Under-21 side. Injury forced him to miss the opening games of Bolton's return to the top flight, but he recovered and won back his midfield spot. However, on New Year's Day 1979, he collided with Everton goalkeeper George Wood on a snow-covered Burnden Park and broke his leg. The game was later abandoned. This time, Reid was missing for 12 months. Contractual problems prevented the midfielder from playing after he failed to agree terms with Arsenal, Everton and Wolverhampton Wanderers. Eventually he was placed on a weekly contract but in September 1981 he broke his leg again in Bolton's match at Barnsley. Again he won his fight for fitness and in December 1982 became one of the bargain buys of all time when Howard Kendall brought him to Goodison Park for £60,000; not that the battle-scarred signing was an overnight sensation. Indeed, initially he seemed to be losing his battle for fitness and Howard Kendall feared the worst. He did recover, however, and soon the Reid option became irresistible; in 1984–85, his most injury-free term, came Everton's finest hour. They came very close to winning the treble of league, FA Cup and European Cup-Winners' Cup and Reid was voted the players' Player of the Year. When he replaced the injured Bryan Robson in the World Cup finals of 1986, the previously ineffective England side took on a new life and there is no doubt that, had he been able to spend less time in plaster, he would have been a major force at international level. From September 1985 ankle trouble limited him to 11 league starts but on his return in February 1987 he proved a telling factor as the Blues won their second league title in three years. On the departure of Howard Kendall in June of that year, he became player-coach, a role he fulfilled until he joined Queens Park Rangers later that year. Following Kendall's appointment as manager of Manchester City, Reid moved to Maine Road as player-coach and in November 1990, following Kendall's return to Goodison Park, he became manager. Once described by Howard Kendall as Everton's most important signing, he is now manager of Sunderland.

RELEGATION. In 110 years as a Football League club, Everton have suffered relegation on only two occasions. The first was in 1929–30, although the club's first four matches – three draws and a 3–0 defeat of Liverpool at Anfield – didn't seem to indicate the problems that lay ahead. After three consecutive defeats, the rot set in and between the beginning of October and the end of March, the club managed only six wins. Aston Villa, Bolton Wanderers and Leicester City all put five goals past them as the Blues crashed to the foot of the table. Sadly, relegation was a foregone conclusion and without three victories in their final three matches of the season things would have been much worse. The club's second experience of relegation came in 1950–51. Before September was out, the Blues had slipped into the relegation zone. They managed to win only one of their last 11 matches and ended the season propping up the division. Relegation was finally decided on goal average, with the bottom three teams all on 32 points, but Everton having scored only 48 goals while conceding 86, were certainties for the drop into the second division.

RICHARDSON, KEVIN. During his time at Goodison Park, the versatile Richardson was never an automatic choice, having to dispute the midfield places with Bracewell, Reid and Sheedy. However, after making his debut as a substitute for Peter Eastoe in a 2–1 home defeat by Sunderland in November 1981, he went on to appear in 139 league and Cup games before being transferred to Watford for £225,000 in September 1986. While he was at Goodison, he appeared in both the League Cup and FA Cup finals of 1984 as well as playing in 15 league games in their championship-winning season of 1984–85. His stay at Vicarage Road was just under a year; he joined Arsenal for £200,000 in August 1987. He won another league championship medal in 1988–89 but at the end of the following season, after a bad injury, he signed for Spanish team Real Sociedad of San Sebastian. In 1991, he returned to England, signing for Aston Villa for £450,000. In his first season he achieved the remarkable record of playing in every minute of all Villa's 51 first-team games, not once being substituted. As team captain, he was ever-present again the following season and played in 102 consecutive league games before missing a match. He deservedly won an England cap against Greece during the 1993–94 season but in February 1995 he followed his old boss Ron Atkinson to Coventry City.

RIDEOUT, PAUL. A much-travelled and experienced striker, Paul Rideout began his career with Swindon Town in 1978. Forty-one goals in 105 matches for the Robins prompted Aston Villa to pay £200,000 for his services in June 1983. In his two seasons at Villa Park, he scored 23 goals in 61 league and Cup games and won five England Under-21 caps but in the summer of 1985 he was sold to Italian club Bari for £400,000. He had a three-year spell in Italy but after Bari were relegated to *Serie B*, he returned to England with Southampton in July 1988 for a fee of £430,000. He netted 23 goals in 93 league and Cup games for the Saints before leaving The Dell for short spells with Swindon Town, Notts County and Glasgow Rangers. Rideout arrived at Goodison in August 1992 and made his debut in a 1–1 home draw against Sheffield Wednesday on the opening day of the season. Although hampered by injuries during his time at Goodison, he was the club's top scorer in 1994–95 with 16 goals including the FA Cup final winner against Manchester United. An unselfish player who holds the ball up well, he has tended to be second-string when Duncan Ferguson is fit.

ROSS, NICK. One of the greatest defenders ever to wear the blue of Everton, Nick Ross played only one season for the club, the Football League's inaugural campaign of 1888–89. He started his career with Hearts but in the summer of 1883 he was given work as a slater in Preston and signed for the Deepdale club. North End soon made him their captain and converted him from a forward to a full-back, one of the game's best. He was in the Preston side that lost to West Bromwich Albion in the FA Cup final of 1888 and missed out on their double-winning season because he joined Everton in the close season. Everton, too, made him their captain and he led the side out for their opening fixture at home to Accrington. He scored five goals in 19 league games that season before rejoining Preston North End and winning a league championship medal in 1889–90. In April 1891, he played for the Football League in their first-ever game. Sadly, Nick Ross, who was never capped by Scotland because they were ignoring players south of the border, died from consumption at the age of 31.

ROSS, TREVOR. Signed from Arsenal for £180,000 in November 1977, the Ashton-under-Lyne midfielder added much needed bite to an Everton side. He made his debut in a 1–0 home win at Derby County but during six years at the club his overall form was inconsistent. He found himself in and out of the side and in February 1983, after scoring 20 goals in 151 league and Cup games, he was given a free transfer. He had loan spells at Portsmouth and Sheffield United as Howard Kendall tried to tempt the Bramall Lane club to part with Terry Curran. Ross was eventually signed by Greek side AEK Athens but the move did not work out and six months later he was back in England having signed for Sheffield United on a permanent basis.

ROYLE, JOE. Widely acknowledged as Everton's finest post-war centre-forward, Joe Royle became the youngest-ever player to wear the famous royal blue when on 15 January 1966, at the age of 16 years 288 days, he played at Blackpool. He had been called in to replace the axed Alex Young but when furious fans attacked manager Harry Catterick, Royle returned to the Central League side. He worked hard at his game to improve his

Joe Royle

clumsy touch on the ball and by the start of the 1967–68 season he had claimed a fully deserved, regular first-team spot. With experience, Royle learnt to time his runs into the penalty area with devastating effect, as he demonstrated in the Blues' 2–1 defeat by Leeds United at Elland Road in November 1968. There seemed to be little danger when Alan Ball clipped in an apparently innocuous cross. Welsh international keeper Gary Sprake was poised to gather it comfortably when Royle appeared from nowhere, horizontal, to glance the ball into the corner of the net. He ended that 1968–69 season as the club's top scorer with 22 league goals and hit his first hat-trick for the club in a 7–1 home win over Leicester City. Royle became a top-class target man, adept at retaining possession under pressure and linking with his fellow attackers. He top-scored for the Blues for the next three seasons, scoring a hat-trick against Southampton at home in September 1969 (4–2) and then four goals against the same opposition in November 1971 as the Saints were beaten 8–0. He was capped ten times at Under-23 level and made his bow for the full England team against Malta in February 1971. He had scored 119 goals in 275 league and Cup games when he was transferred to Manchester City for £200,000 in December 1974. He scored 31 goals in 117 league and Cup games for the Maine Road club before moving to Bristol City for £90,000 in November 1977. After three years at Ashton Gate, he joined Norwich City where his playing career came to a premature end because of injury. Entering management with Oldham Athletic, he combined integrity, humour and sound judgement as the Latics won promotion from the second division and reached the League Cup final and FA Cup semi-finals. In November 1994, he returned to Goodison as manager. His first game in charge was the club's most eagerly anticipated confrontation of the season, the Merseyside derby against Liverpool at Goodison Park. The Blues triumphed 2–0 with Duncan Ferguson, whom Royle signed from Glasgow Rangers, scoring one of the goals. He kept the club in the Premier League but in March 1997, after clashes with chairman Peter Johnson over transfer deals, Royle quit the Goodison club by mutual consent. After a spell out of the game, he is now manager of Manchester City.

RUMBELOWS CUP. See Football League Cup.

RUNNERS-UP. Everton have been first division runners-up on seven occasions – 1889–90, 1894–95, 1901–2, 1904–5, 1908–9, 1911–12 and 1985–86.

S

SAGAR, TED. One of the greatest goalkeepers of all-time, Ted Sagar's career as an Everton player spanned over 24 years during which time he played in 495 league and Cup games. Had the war not intervened, that figure would have been considerably higher. Sagar joined the Blues from Thorne Colliery in March 1929 after a trial with Hull City and stayed with the club until retiring in May 1953. He made his Everton debut in a 4–0 home win over Derby County on 18 January 1930 and his last league appearance in a 1–0 defeat at Plymouth Argyle on 15 November 1952. Combining sheer athleticism with bravery and tremendous vision, Sagar's handling, particularly of crosses, was exemplary. It was his misfortune to have been a contemporary of Harry Hibbs and Vic Woodley, otherwise he would have won far more than the four England caps that came his way. He won league championship medals in 1932 and 1939 and was in goal when the Blues defeated Manchester City in the FA Cup final of 1933. Slim and perhaps even underweight for a goalkeeper in the days when it was legitimate for centre-forwards to bounce both keeper and ball into the net, Sagar survived by skill alone. He had the uncanny ability to judge the high flight of a ball and was completely without nerves. Famous for launching himself headlong at the ball, regardless of the number of players blocking his path, he made his farewell appearance against Tranmere Rovers in the Liverpool Senior Cup final.

SAUNDERS, GEORGE. Recommended to Everton by Dixie Dean, full-back George Saunders made his debut in wartime football against Liverpool on 2 December 1939. His next game for the club was his league debut seven years later when he played in the 3–2 home win

Ted Sagar

over Arsenal on 11 September 1946. More than useful in the air, Saunders was a strong, hard-tackling defender with a mighty clearance. He played the last of his 140 first-team games in a 5–1 home defeat by Notts County during the 1951–52 season.

SCANDAL. On 11 April 1964, *The People* newspaper carried a sensational story claiming that Tony Kay, the Everton captain, along with two former colleagues at Sheffield Wednesday, had accepted bribes to throw a match between Wednesday and Ipswich Town in 1962. The Goodison Park club were stunned. Kay was immediately suspended. He was charged, tried with several others and sent to prison. As a result, he was banned from playing football for life. Harry Catterick had paid Sheffield Wednesday £60,000 for Kay who had played in only 55 games for the Blues. More importantly, Catterick felt the player had been unfairly punished. Losing Kay was obviously a severe blow to the club's title aspirations, but worse was to come. With the 1964–65 season about to start, *The People* published another exposé. The newspaper claimed that certain Everton players had been taking drugs to improve their performances. The Goodison board immediately ordered a thorough investigation and although they uncovered nothing, another terrible stigma had been attached to the club.

150

SCHOOL OF SCIENCE. This was the nickname given to Everton in the 1930s in acknowledgement of the team's premeditated and precise style of play. The side established itself as one of the strongest of its day, carrying off the second and first division championships in successive seasons, 1930–31 and 1931–32.

SCOTT, ALEX. After a very successful career with Glasgow Rangers, with whom he won a Scottish League championship medal, two Scottish League Cup winners' medals and a Scottish Cup final medal, Alex Scott joined Everton in February 1963. The winger was already established as a regular in the Scottish national side when he made it known that he would like to play south of the border. Everton's main rivals for his signature were Tottenham Hotspur but it was Harry Catterick who won the day with a £40,000 bid. Scott made his debut in a 3–1 defeat at Leicester City, one of only six matches the club lost that season as they won the first division championship. He went on to win an FA Cup winners' medal in 1966 but in September 1967, after he had scored 26 goals in 176 league and Cup games, he returned to his native Scotland to play for Hibernian.

SCOTT, BILLY. Irish international goalkeeper Billy Scott joined Everton from Linfield in 1904 and immediately succeeded the legendary Dick Roose. He made his debut in a 2–1 win at Notts County on the opening day of the 1904–5 season and over the next eight seasons hardly missed a game. At the end of his first season, he won a league championship runners-up medal, a feat he repeated in seasons 1908–9 and 1911–12. He was also Everton's goalkeeper in their 1906 and 1907 FA Cup final appearances and during his Goodison career was capped 16 times by Ireland. The brother of Liverpool's Elisha, he left Everton in the summer of 1912, after playing in 289 league and Cup games, to join Leeds City.

SCREEN SPORTS CUP. In 1985–86, the Blues took part in the Screen Sports Super Cup. Playing in the same group as Manchester United and Norwich City, Everton qualified for the semi-final stages of the competition by beating Manchester United 4–2 at Old Trafford and 1–0 at Goodison Park where an own goal by Frank Stapleton separated the teams. A Gary Lineker goal gave the Blues a 1–0 home win over Norwich City but at Carrow Road, the Canaries won 1–0. In the semi-final first leg, Neville Southall performed heroics in a goalless draw against Spurs at White Hart Lane. In the return, goals from Heath, Mountfield and Sharp gave the Blues a 3–1 win. The final against Liverpool was held over to the start of the following season and with Lineker having left for Barcelona, Everton lost 3–1 at Anfield and 4–1 at Goodison Park.

SECOND DIVISION. Everton's first season in the second division was 1930–31. Determined that their stay would only be a short one, the Blues won their opening match at Plymouth Argyle 3–2. In the New Year, they put together a record-breaking run of ten wins, scoring 43 goals. The title was won before spring had arrived and Everton eased up, losing three of their final five games. It didn't really matter as they finished seven points ahead of their nearest rivals and scored a phenomenal 121 goals in the process. The club's second spell in the second division came in August 1951 after relegation the previous season. At one stage, relegation to the third division (North) was staring them in the face, but the club's fortunes improved and they ended the season in seventh place. In 1952–53, the Blues finished in 16th place, five points clear of relegation, beating Doncaster Rovers 7–1 but losing 8–2 at Huddersfield Town on the way. The club's final season in the second division was 1953–54 when they notched up 11 games without defeat. They ended the season as runners-up to Leicester City, one point ahead of Blackburn Rovers.

SEMI-FINALS. Up to the end of the 1997–98 season, Everton had been involved in 23 FA Cup semi-finals and three Football League Cup semi-finals.

SETTLE, JIMMY. Jimmy Settle began his career with Bolton Wanderers before moving on to Bury, but it was with Everton that his career took off. He joined the club towards the end of the 1898–99 season and made his debut in the penultimate game of the campaign, a goalless draw at Burnley. A classy inside-forward whose defence-splitting passes were a feature of his game, Settle also scored his fair share of goals, netting 97 in 269 league and Cup appearances. His best season was 1901–2 when he scored 18 goals in 29 league games, including a hat-trick in a 6–1 home win over Wolverhampton Wanderers. His only other hat-trick came in an FA Cup third-round tie in 1904–5 when Southampton were beaten 4–0 at Goodison Park. Settle was capped six times by England between 1899 and 1903 and played in the 1906 and 1907 FA Cup finals before leaving the Blues to end his career with Stockport County.

SHARP, GRAEME. A virtually unknown striker when Gordon Lee paid Dumbarton £120,000 for his services in April 1980, Graeme Sharp made his debut as a substitute in a goalless draw at Brighton a month later. He

Graeme Sharp

took a while to settle down at Goodison and even considered moving on, but when Howard Kendall was appointed manager his career began to blossom. He enjoyed a series of fruitful combinations, first with Adrian Heath, then Andy Gray and finally Gary Lineker. Tall and strong, Sharp was an aerial playmaker who combined power and deftness and was able to distribute the ball as accurately with his head as his contemporaries could with their feet. He was the scorer of the club's first goal in the 2–0 FA Cup final victory over Watford in 1984 and the following season scored 30 goals. He headed the equaliser against Bayern Munich in the 1984–85 European Cup-Winners' Cup semi-final and his rise to stardom saw him capped by Scotland's manager Jock Stein in his country's first full World Cup qualifier against Iceland in May of that year. Sharp's most spectacular strike came at Anfield on 20 October 1984. Gary Stevens sent a long high pass out of defence that dropped obligingly into the Scotsman's path; he took it down on his left instep, wrong-footed Mark Lawrenson in the process and as the ball sat up perfectly for him, he hit a dipping 25-yard right-foot volley over the picturesque leap of Bruce Grobbelaar to give the Blues a 1–0 win in the Merseyside derby. In July 1991, Sharp joined Oldham Athletic for £500,000. Although he was 30 and his goal tally had deteriorated in recent seasons, he was the club's top post-war goalscorer with 150 goals in 432 league and Cup appearances and there were those who reckoned he was released too soon. He later became Oldham manager when Joe Royle returned to Goodison Park but resigned his post in February 1997.

SHARP, JACK. Hereford-born Jack Sharp played his early football with local club Hereford Thistle before signing for Aston Villa in 1897. Unable to win a regular first-team place at Villa Park, he joined Everton in 1899 and after making his debut in a 2–1 home defeat by Sheffield United in the opening game of the 1899–1900 season, went on to give the club 11 seasons' service. The Yorkshire side were also Everton's opposition when Sharp scored his only hat–trick for the club in a 3–2 win for the Blues on 10 February 1906. Sharp played in Everton's FA Cup finals in 1906 and 1907, picking up a winners' medal in the first as Newcastle United were beaten 1–0, and scoring the goal as they lost 2–1 to Sheffield Wednesday in the second. In 1903, Sharp won the first of his two full caps for England when he played against Ireland. He went on to score 80 goals for Everton in 342 league and Cup games before concentrating on cricket. He played for Lancashire from 1899 to 1925, captaining them for a time, and scored 22,015 runs at an average of 31.18. He hit 36 centuries, with a highest score of 211 against Leicestershire. Also a fast-medium bowler, he took 434 wickets at 27.23 and held 223 catches. Sharp was a double international, playing in three Tests for England and scoring 105 against Australia at The Oval in 1909.

SHEEDY, KEVIN. Kevin Sheedy began his career with Hereford United before joining Liverpool in the summer of 1978. Despite his outstanding Central League form for the Reds, he was restricted to just two first-team appearances in four years and in June 1982 he joined Everton for £100,000. The young Irishman made his debut for the Blues in a 2–0 defeat at Watford on the opening day of the 1982–83 season and soon went on to prove what a bargain buy he was. One of the finest left-sided midfield players that the Goodison club has ever had, he was a major influence on the Everton side that won two league titles in the mid-1980s. Sheedy scored some useful goals, such as the third in the 1985 European Cup-Winners' Cup final victory over Rapid Vienna, and some spectacular ones from free-kicks that would find their way into the top corner from 30 yards and beyond. A Republic of Ireland international, winning 45 full caps, he left Goodison in February 1992 after scoring 92 goals in 351 league and Cup games. He had suffered with injuries towards the end of his Everton career but went on to play for both Newcastle United and Blackpool before hanging up his boots.

Kevin Sheedy

SHEFFIELD WEDNESDAY. Everton and Sheffield Wednesday have been drawn together more times in the FA Cup than any other two clubs in history. They have clashed in 14 ties including two finals, Wednesday winning the first of those 2–1 in 1907 and Everton the second 3–2 in 1966. The results of these meetings are as follows:

Date	Venue	Stage	Score
18.02.1893	Goodison Park	Round 3	3–0
2.03.95	Olive Grove	Round 3	0–2
29.02.96	Olive Grove	Round 3	0–4
10.03.06	Goodison Park	Round 4	4–3
20.04.07	Crystal Palace	Final	1–2
29.01.21	Goodison Park	Round 3	1–1
3.02.21	Hillsborough	Round 3r	1–0
30.01.37	Goodison Park	Round 4	3–0
25.01.47	Hillsborough	Round 4	1–2

Date	Venue	Stage	Score
20.02.54	Hillsborough	Round 5	1–3
9.01.65	Goodison Park	Round 3	2–2
13.01.65	Hillsborough	Round 3r	3–0
14.05.66	Wembley	Final	3–2
5.04.86	Villa Park	Semi-final	2–1
9.01.88	Hillsborough	Round 3	1–1
13.01.88	Goodison Park	Round 3r	1–1
25.01.88	Goodison Park	Round 3rr	1–1
27.01.88	Hillsborough	Round 3rrr	5–0
28.01.90	Hillsborough	Round 4	2–1

SHORT, CRAIG. The Bridlington-born defender played for Pickering Town and England Schools before joining Scarborough at the age of 19. He made his league debut against Hereford United and appeared in 63 league games for the club before moving to Notts County for £100,000 in July 1989. He played for the Meadow Lane side for three seasons, including the second division play-off final success against Brighton in 1991. In September 1992, he joined Derby County for a record £2.5 million, preferring the Rams to Blackburn Rovers. A strong, tall and imposing centre-back, Short played in 136 league and Cup games for County before signing for Everton in the 1995 close season. Despite an unconvincing debut against Nottingham Forest, he soon began to find the accomplished form that had alerted Joe Royle in the first place. Short struck up a good understanding with fellow defender Dave Watson and has provided a constant threat from set-pieces with his heading ability. Short's first European outing ended in disgrace in Rotterdam when he was sent off in the final minute of a Cup-Winners' Cup tie against Feyenoord for elbowing former Dutch international Ronald Koeman.

SIMOD CUP. The Simod Cup replaced the Full Members' Cup from the 1987–88 season. In the Blues' first match in the newly named competition, they went down 2–1 at home to Luton Town with Paul Power netting the Everton goal. In 1988–89, the Blues went all the way to the final. After disposing of Millwall (home 2–0) and Wimbledon (away 2–1), they beat Queens Park Rangers 1–0 in the semi-final with Pat Nevin scoring the all-important winner. In a most thrilling final, Everton went down 4–3 to Nottingham Forest after extra-time with Tony Cottee (2) and Graeme Sharp scoring for the Goodison club.

SMITH, WALTER. Appointed Everton manager in the summer of 1998, Walter Smith won his first Scottish Championship at Rangers in 1991 after only four games in charge! The former Dundee United player went from strength to strength, winning again in 1992, 1993, 1994, 1995, 1996 and 1997 and up until last season was the only manager in Scottish football – perhaps even world football – to have never finished a season with his club without the League Championship safely in the cabinet.

SNODIN, IAN. The younger brother of Glynn, Ian Snodin followed in his footsteps by joining Doncaster Rovers as an associated schoolboy in 1979. He spent six years at Belle Vue as the Yorkshire side yo-yoed between the third and fourth divisions but after making 212 first-team appearances he joined Leeds United for £200,000. Immediately appointed club captain, Snodin was at Elland Road for less than two years before Everton's manager, Howard Kendall, added him to his title-chasing side in January 1987 for a fee of £840,000. Having turned down the chance to join Liverpool to sign for the Blues, Snodin played throughout the final four months of the season to win a league championship medal. In March 1989, an injury he received in a league match against Sheffield Wednesday prevented his selection for England against Albania and kept him out of the Everton side that lost 3–2 to Liverpool in the FA Cup final. Although he was never able to shrug off his injury problems fully, he went on to appear in 200 first-team games for the Blues before joining Oldham Athletic on a free transfer in January 1995.

SOUTHALL, NEVILLE. Between leaving school and becoming a full-time footballer, Neville Southall spent six years working as a dustman, a mopper-up in a café and a hod carrier on a building site. While living in Llandudno, he kept goal for both Bangor City and Conwy United but it was his fine form at Winsford United that caused Bury to pay £6,000 for him in June 1980. In the summer of 1981, after only 44 first-team appearances for the Gigg Lane club, he signed for Everton in a £150,000 deal. He made his debut for the Blues on 17 October 1981 in a 2–1 win over Ipswich Town. Things didn't go too smoothly for him after that, for after a 5–0 home defeat against Liverpool, he was dropped and sent on loan to Port Vale. After nine games he returned to Goodison and was ever-present for the remainder of that and the next two seasons as his and Everton's form improved beyond all expectations. Two outstanding saves against John Barnes contributed greatly to the club's 1984 FA Cup final victory over Watford, and during the next few seasons, Southall established a peerless reputation.

Neville Southall

In 1985 he was voted the Football Writers' Player of the Year and no less an authority than former Northern Ireland international keeper Pat Jennings described him as a keeper without a weakness. His anticipation is superb and he is a magnificent shot-stopper but what gives him the edge is an astonishing capacity to change direction at the last moment, sometimes even in mid-air, and an instinct for improvising unorthodox saves. His part in one bizarre incident – a goalmouth sit-in after walking out of a half-time harangue by Everton manager Colin Harvey – did the big Welshman less than credit, even though Southall is his own man and he was acting out of frustration rather than malice. Southall has won 91 Welsh caps, and holds Everton's club record for league appearances, passing Ted Sagar's previous record, with 566 under his belt. After a spell on loan with Stoke City, he joined the Potters on a permanent basis.

SOUTHWORTH, JACK. Jack Southworth was just 16 years of age when he scored six goals in a match against Leigh whilst playing for Blackburn Olympic. Moving to Blackburn Rovers, he won FA Cup winners' medals in 1890 and 1891. In 1892, a floodlit testimonial match was arranged for him against Darwen. He had scored a remarkable 103 goals in 107 league games when, in the summer of 1893, Everton paid £400 to bring him to Goodison Park. He scored on his debut but the Blues lost 7–3 at Derby County and, although it took a while for this prolific goalscorer to settle at his new club, he eventually began to pile in the goals. He scored four in an 8–1 home win over Sheffield Wednesday and six in the next match, a 7–1 defeat of West Bromwich Albion, again at Goodison. Not surprisingly, he ended the season as the club's top scorer with 27 goals in 22 games. In 1894–95, he had scored nine goals in his first nine matches, including hat-tricks against Small Heath (home 5–0) and Nottingham Forest (home 6–1) when injury forced him into premature retirement. Whilst with Blackburn Rovers he had made three appearances for England, scoring three goals and was unfortunate to be playing at a time when Bloomer, Goodall, Lindley and G.O. Smith were on the scene. A man of immense talent, Southworth became a professional violinist, good enough to play with the Hallé Orchestra.

SPEED, GARY. Beginning his career with Leeds United, Gary Speed made his first-team debut in the penultimate game of the 1988–89 season in a 0–0 draw against Oldham Athletic at Elland Road. It was midway through the following season, when Leeds won the second division championship, that Speed got an extended run in the team, his form earning him a full Welsh cap against Costa Rica. He played in all but one game of Leeds' victorious league championship campaign in 1991–92 and scored several vital goals. Although operating in many positions, including striker, central defender and full-back, it is in his more customary role on the left-hand side of midfield that he is happiest. He had scored 55 goals in 295 league and Cup games for Leeds when, in June 1996, he joined Everton in a five-year deal for £3.5 million. Speed scored on his debut in a 2–0 home win over Newcastle United and went on to play in 37 of the 38 league games that season. He scored nine goals in the Premiership, including a hat-trick in a 7–1 home win over Southampton. Capped over 40 times by Wales, Speed left Goodison in January 1998 to join Newcastle United after a much-publicised bust-up which resulted in him refusing to travel to the club's game at Upton Park.

SPONSORS. The club's present sponsors are one 2 one. Everton's previous sponsors were Danka Copiers and Fax Machines, NEC and Hafnia.

ST DOMINGO'S. Some churches in the area had organised football teams as early as the 1870s with St Benedict's, St John's of Bootle and St Peter's the first to field sides. It wasn't until towards the end of that decade that the Rev B.S. Chambers became minister of St Domingo and his enthusiasm for sport led to the formation of a cricket club for Church and Sunday School members in 1876. A couple of years later, a football section was formed for the winter months; thus the first steps were taken towards creating what was to become Everton Football Club. St Domingo's Football Club kicked off in a corner of nearby Stanley Park, with games against various church sides. The team quickly attracted outsiders who wanted to play. It was decided that the team should change its name in order to accommodate non-church members more reasonably. At a meeting at the Queen's Head Hotel, Village Street in November 1879, the name of the district Everton was chosen.

STEIN, JIMMY. Born in Coatbridge, Jimmy Stein helped Dunfermline gain promotion to the Scottish first division before joining Everton in 1928. Quite a prolific scorer for a winger, he netted four in Everton's 9–1 win over Plymouth Argyle on 27 December 1930 as they went on to win the second division championship. He won a league championship winners' medal in 1931–32 and the following season had his best campaign in terms of goals scored, hitting 21 in 46 league and Cup games. That season the Blues won the FA Cup with Stein netting the first of Everton's goals in the final, which ended in a 3–0 win over Manchester City. Never one to complain if he was left out of the side to accommodate a younger player, Stein scored 65 goals in 215 league and Cup games before joining Burnley in October 1936. Later he returned to Merseyside to help New Brighton.

STEVEN, TREVOR. Beginning his league career with Burnley, Trevor Steven earned rave reviews game after game and soon had the bigger clubs tracking his progress. In the summer of 1983, within a week of the arrival of the new Burnley management team of John Bond and John Benson, Steven was on his way to Everton for a fee of £325,000. Although he wasn't a regular in his first season at Goodison Park, he collected an FA Cup winners' medal in 1984 as Watford were defeated in the Wembley final. The following year, the league title was secured by Everton, with Steven's silky skills and tight control complementing the more aggressive combative style of Peter Reid. In addition, the Blues won the European Cup-Winners' Cup, defeating Rapid Vienna 3–1 in the final in Rotterdam. Steven chipped in with a goal, as he had

Trevor Steven

done in the deciding leg of the semi-final against Bayern Munich at Goodison Park. Steven had by now become a full England international, winning his first cap in the World Cup qualifier against Northern Ireland in Belfast in February 1985. He played for England in the final stages of the 1986 World Cup. In Everton's league championship-winning campaign of 1986–87 Steven scored 14 goals. After playing for Everton against Liverpool in the 1989 FA Cup final, Steven refused to sign a new contract and joined Glasgow Rangers for a fee of £1.5 million. With the Ibrox club, he won two league championship medals and a League Cup winners' medal but in August 1991 he was surprisingly sold to Marseille for £5.5 million. In his only season on the Riviera, the French club won the championship, then sold Steven back to Rangers for £2.4 million. He won two more league championship medals and a further two League Cup-winners' medals but after the last success he was no longer an automatic choice.

STEVENS, GARY. Joining Everton straight from school, Gary Stevens made such an impact in the club's Central League side that he was

Gary Stevens

given his first-team debut in a 1–1 draw at West Ham United in October 1981. However, it was another 12 months before he gained a regular place in the Everton line-up, replacing Brian Borrows. His great composure on the ball allied to his natural sprinting ability led to his call-up to the full England squad for the World Cup qualifier against Northern Ireland in February 1985, although it was later that year when he made his full debut against World Cup holders Italy in Mexico. A member of the England team which reached the 1986 World Cup quarter-finals, he went on to appear in 46 games for his country. For Everton, he won two league championship medals, an FA Cup winners' medal and a European Cup-Winners' Cup medal. After appearing in 284 league and Cup games, he left Goodison in the 1988 close season to sign for Glasgow Rangers for a fee of £1.25 million. At Ibrox, he won six Scottish Premier Division championship medals, a Scottish Cup winners' medal and three Scottish League Cup medals. In September 1994, after appearing in 245 first-team games for the Scottish giants, he returned to Merseyside to play for Tranmere

Rovers. His versatility and experience has proved an invaluable asset at Prenton Park, where he has clocked up more than 100 league appearances.

STEVENSON, ALEX. Born in Dublin, Alex Stevenson won the first of his Republic of Ireland caps in 1932 with the Dolphin club, but he made his name in Scotland with Glasgow Rangers. In fact, his love for the Ibrox club was such that it took a great deal of persuasion for Stevenson to leave Rangers and join Everton. After making his debut for the Blues in a 2–1 win at Arsenal in February 1934, he went on to form a good partnership with fellow Irishman Jackie Coulter. In the five seasons leading up to the Second World War, Stevenson scored 77 goals in 254 games, including two goals in a match on ten occasions. One of the game's finest ball-players, he continued to play in the Everton side after the hostilities had ended, playing the last of 271 games, in which he scored 90 goals, against Bolton Wanderers on the final day of the 1948–49 season. Stevenson was capped 17 times for Northern Ireland and seven times for the Republic of Ireland.

STEWART, BILLY. One of the main features of Billy Stewart's play was his exceptionally long throw-in, although his running and jumping technique was eventually outlawed. He first came to the fore when playing with the Black Watch team which won the Army Cup. Later, while stationed with the Royal Scots Greys in Ireland, he was a member of the Belfast Distillery side which won the Irish Cup. Preston North End bought him out of the army in 1890 and in three seasons with the Deepdale club, he made 70 league appearances. He joined Everton in the summer of 1893 and made his debut in a 3–2 home defeat by Sheffield United on the opening day of the 1893–94 season. Forming part of Everton's famous half-back line of Holt, Campbell and Stewart, he played in the 1897 FA Cup final which the Blues lost 3–2 to Aston Villa. Midway through the following season he left Goodison after playing in 137 league and Cup games for the Blues to become captain of Bristol City as they began to establish themselves as a professional club.

STUART, GRAHAM. Graham Stuart joined Chelsea from the FA School of Excellence in the summer of 1989 and made his first-team debut at the end of the 1989–90 season, scoring in a 3–0 win over Crystal Palace. He scored 14 goals in 87 games for the Stamford Bridge club before Mike Walker brought him to Goodison for £850,000 in August 1993. An England Under–21 international, Stuart made his Everton debut in a 4–2 home win over Sheffield United. In the final game of the season against Wimbledon, he scored two goals, including an 81st-minute winner after the Blues had been two goals down, which saved the club from relegation. The London-born player didn't get much chance to shine, but an injury to Vinny Samways gave him a place in the victorious FA Cup final side of 1995. Able to play on either wing or in a more advanced striking role, Stuart went on to score 28 goals in 141 league and Cup games before being transferred to Sheffield United.

SUBSTITUTES. Everton's first substitute was John Hurst, who came on for Fred Pickering in the club's third game of the 1965–66 season, a 1–1 draw against Stoke City at the Victoria Ground. The club's first goalscoring Number 12 was Sandy Brown who scored in Everton's 3–1 home win over Liverpool on 27 August 1966. The greatest number of substitutes used in a single season by the Blues under the single-substitute rule was 30 in 1980–81. From 1986–87, two substitutes were allowed and in 1992–93, the club used 69, still the highest despite three substitutes being allowed for the past few seasons. The greatest number of substitute appearances for the Blues has been made by Stuart Barlow, who came on during 47 league games, including an extraordinary 18 league appearances in the substitute's shirt during the 1992–93 season.

SUNDAY FOOTBALL. The first-ever Sunday matches in the Football League took place on 20 January 1974 during the three-day week imposed by the government during its trial of strength with the coal-miners. Everton had to wait until the following Sunday, 27 January, before playing their first game on the Sabbath – a fourth-round FA Cup tie at home to West Bromwich Albion that ended goalless. Since then, the club have played numerous games on a Sunday, including both the Simod Cup and Zenith Data Systems Cup finals.

SUSTAINED SCORING. The man who scored the highest number of goals for Everton in a league match was Jack Southworth. He hit six in a 7–1 win over West Bromwich Albion on 30 December 1893. A week earlier he had scored four times in an 8–1 win over Sheffield Wednesday and between 9 December 1893 and 13 January 1894, he registered 16 goals in seven games. He played 22 games that season and scored 27 goals. Bertie Freeman created a first division record in 1908–9 when he scored 36 goals in 37 appearances including a spell of 17 in ten consecutive games. The feat was equalled in 1914–15 when

Bobby Parker scored 36 goals in 35 games, including six hat-tricks. The great Dixie Dean scored the unsurpassable total of 60 league goals in 39 games in 1927–28. He scored 17 in the first nine games of the season and 15 in the last seven. In 1930–31 he scored 39 goals in 37 matches including a spell of 23 goals in 12 consecutive games.

T

TAYLOR, JACK. One of the most versatile players of his day, Jack Taylor first played for Dumbarton Athletic before signing for St Mirren. He joined Everton in the summer of 1896 and made his debut in the opening game of the 1896–97 season, scoring the winning goal in a 2–1 home defeat of Sheffield Wednesday. Operating mainly on the right-wing that season, he was the club's second-top scorer with 13 league goals, including a hat-trick in a 4–1 win at West Bromwich Albion. He appeared in the FA Cup final at the end of that season and when the club returned to the Crystal Palace in 1906 and 1907, he was the sole playing survivor from the Everton side that lost 3–2 to Aston Villa in 1897. A most inspirational footballer, he went on to appear in 456 league and Cup games for Everton over 14 seasons with the club, his career being effectively brought to an end by a freak accident. In the FA Cup semi-final replay against Barnsley at Old Trafford in March 1910, he was hit in the throat by a fierce shot and sustained severe damage to his larynx. It was an injury from which the popular Taylor never really recovered and at the end of the season he left Goodison to join non-league South Liverpool.

TELEVISION. In 1936, Everton took part in the first football match to be shown on television when a film of their match against Arsenal on 29 August was shown on the BBC. Everton's first appearance on BBC's *Match of the Day* was on 31 October 1964 when they went down 3–1 against Arsenal at Highbury in a first division game with Fred Pickering scoring for the Toffees. When Everton were drawn at home to neighbours Liverpool in the FA Cup fifth round in March 1967, they were approached by a company offering to cover the game on closed-circuit television with large screens being erected at Anfield. This was a unique occasion, for a crowd of 64,851 paid for admission to see the game live at Goodison Park, whilst 40,149 were present at Anfield to watch the game on television. The combined attendance of 105,000 created a new record for an FA Cup tie apart from a final and has never been beaten. For the record, the tie was decided in Everton's favour by an Alan Ball goal in the closing moments of the first half. When the two clubs met in the FA Cup semi-final on 23 April 1977, the game stood at 2–2 with three minutes to go. Ronnie Goodlass crossed from the left, McKenzie helped it on and substitute Bryan Hamilton nudged the ball past Ray Clemence from the six-yard line. Everton celebrated what everybody in the ground believed was the winning goal – everybody that is, except Welsh referee Clive Thomas. He awarded a free-kick against Hamilton, saying that there had been an infringement. Jimmy Hill's analysis was inconclusive as the ball went into the net off Hamilton's hip and when McKenzie played the ball, he was fractionally behind Joey Jones. Everton and Liverpool played at Goodison Park on 28 October 1978 in what was the BBC's *Match of the Season*. The Blues beat Liverpool 1–0 to record their first success in seven years. Everton's goalscorer was Andy King, who along with an interviewer was pushed off the pitch by a policeman after the game. The BBC's *Sportsnight* cameras captured Everton's win at Oxford United when a Kevin Brock pass was intercepted by Adrian Heath and, in one moment, the club's season was transformed. They reached two Wembley finals and beat Watford to lift the FA Cup. Graeme Sharp's goal on 20 October 1984, that meant Everton beat Liverpool 1–0, was one of the finest seen on *Match of the Day*. He controlled the ball on his left foot with one touch and then, with his right, volleyed an unstoppable shot past Grobbelaar from outside the penalty area.

TELFER, GEORGE. After making his Everton debut in a 1–0 defeat at Arsenal in December 1973, speedy winger George Telfer's form was so impressive that he was talked about as an England international of the future. Lethal inside the penalty area, he scored a number of spectacular goals for the Blues, especially the two in the 3–0 home win over Wolves in February 1976. It was only after the arrival of Duncan McKenzie from Anderlecht in December of that year that Telfer lost his first-team place, but despite offers from a number of clubs, he decided to stay at Goodison and fight to get it back. However, his appearances over the next few seasons were few and far between and at the end of the 1980–81 season, after scoring 22 goals in 113 appearances, he left to play for San Diego in the NASL. He later returned to England to play for Scunthorpe United and then Preston North End before entering non-league football with Runcorn and Barrow.

TEMPLE, DEREK. Having played for Lancashire and England Schoolboys, Derek Temple joined Everton shortly after leaving school. His form with the colts side was amazing; in one season alone, the Liverpool-born forward scored 70 goals, including six in one match. His form was such that he made his first-team debut at the age of 18 against Newcastle United at Goodison in March 1957. He played in seven games at the end of that season, scoring three goals including one in his second game, a 2–2 draw at Sheffield Wednesday. In 1965, he was capped by England and played against West Germany in Nuremberg. The following season he won a place in Everton's 'Hall of Fame' when he scored the winning goal in the Blues' marvellous 3–2 win over Sheffield Wednesday in the FA Cup final at Wembley. Temple went on to score 82 goals in 273 league and Cup games for Everton, including a hat-trick in a 5–2 home win over Ipswich Town in September 1961. In September 1967, he was transferred to Preston North End for £35,000 and played in 76 league games for the Deepdale club before joining then non-league Wigan Athletic.

TEXACO CUP. The predecessor of the Anglo-Scottish Cup, the Texaco Cup was launched in 1970–71 and was for English, Irish and Scottish club sides not involved in European competitions that season. In 1973–74, Everton went out of the competition without scoring a goal, losing 1–0 to Heart of Midlothian at Goodison Park and drawing 0–0 at Tynecastle.

THOMAS, DAVE. After making his name with Burnley, for whom the speedy winger scored 23 goals in 179 first-team games, Dave Thomas opted to join Queens Park Rangers, despite the interest shown by Everton, Leeds United and Manchester United. He signed for the Loftus Road club for a fee of £165,000 in October 1972 and enjoyed five successful seasons with the London club, including winning eight full international caps for England. Everton were one of a number of clubs interested in signing Thomas in the summer of 1977, when the Liverpool-born winger wanted to move back north, and they eventually completed the transfer in August of that year for a fee of £200,000. Making his debut in a 3–1 defeat at home to Nottingham Forest on the opening day of the 1977–78 season, Thomas provided the crosses from which Bob Latchford scored 30 goals. However, he stayed only for two seasons at Goodison before leaving to join Wolverhampton Wanderers. Never really settling at Molineux, he had a spell with Vancouver Whitecaps in the NASL before returning to these shores to play for Middlesbrough. Thomas ended his league career with Portsmouth where he became youth-team coach.

THOMSON, JOCK. Born in Thornton, Fife, left-half Jock Thomson joined Everton from Dundee in March 1930 and made his debut at the end of the month in a 2–1 home defeat by West Ham United. In 1930–31, he played in 41 league games as the Blues won the second division championship and a year later was an important member of Everton's league championship-winning team. In 1932–33, he scored his first goals for the club and helped Everton win the FA Cup. That season also saw him win his only Scottish cap against Wales at Tynecastle. An ever-present in 1934–35, Thomson lost his place to the young Joe Mercer but after Cliff Britton retired and Mercer switched to right-half, Thomson returned to the team and in 1938–39 won another league championship medal. He hung up his boots in 1939 after scoring five goals in 294 games for the Goodison club. From 1947 to 1950 he was manager of Manchester City.

TRANSFERS. The club's record transfer fee received is the £8 million that Italian club Fiorentina paid for Andrei Kanchelskis in February 1997. Everton's record transfer fee paid is £5.75 million to Middlesbrough for Nick Barmby in October 1996.

TREBILCOCK, MIKE. Virtually unknown when he joined the club from Plymouth Argyle for £20,000 on the last day of 1965, Mike Trebilcock went on to carve a place for himself in the club's history. After replacing Fred Pickering in the Blues' 1–0 FA Cup semi-final win over Manchester United at Bolton's Burnden Park, he surprisingly kept his place for the final against Sheffield Wednesday. Everton were trailing 2–0 when, after 59 minutes, Trebilcock shot past Springett after Temple's header had been blocked. Five minutes later, the Cornishman fired Everton level after Alex Scott's free-kick had only been partially cleared. Then of course, with ten minutes to play, Derek Temple scored the goal to give Everton perhaps their most famous victory. It was Trebilcock's last Cup game for the club. In fact, in two years at Goodison he played in only 14 league and Cup games and in January 1968 he was allowed to join Portsmouth. He scored 36 goals in 122 games for the Fratton Park club before ending his league career with Torquay United and then emigrating to Australia.

TROUP, ALEC. Alec Troup began his career with his home-town club Forfar Athletic before joining Dundee. It was from the Dens Park club that Everton signed him in January 1923. Standing only 5ft 5ins, the tiny Scottish winger made his debut in a 4–1 defeat at Stoke that month and went on to appear in the 17 games that remained of that campaign. He had won four Scottish caps before he came to Goodison and added another in 1926 when he played against England. Troup had a weak collarbone and had to have it heavily strapped before every game, yet despite this, he was able to provide many of the pin-point crosses that hung in the air for Dixie Dean to convert in his 1927–28 haul of 60 league goals. Troup, too, had his best season in terms of goals scored in that campaign, netting ten as an ever-present. In 1930, after scoring 35 goals in 259 league and Cup games, he left Goodison and rejoined Dundee.

TURNSTILE FRAUD. During the 1895–96 season, suspicions had been voiced that the estimated crowds and the turnstile returns did not tally. For the match against Sunderland on 12 December 1895, a director and groundsman noted the number at which the turnstile would start half-an-hour before the gates were opened as usual. However, when the numbers were checked again by two directors some 20 minutes later, they were found to have been moved back by 200 units. The 'Everton Turnstile Fraud' was a sensation of the day and about 15 conspirators, including the groundsman, appeared in court.

U

UEFA CUP. Unfortunately, the Blues were drawn against top Italian side AC Milan in the first round of the 1975–76 UEFA Cup competition. After a goalless draw at Goodison, the side travelled to Itlay for the second leg and, although they put up a brave fight, they went out of the competition to a single Milan goal. Three years later, the club were back in Europe and were drawn against Irish club Finn Harps. Two goals from Andy King helped the Blues to a 5–0 win in Ireland and then the Goodison club repeated the scoreline at home to go through 10–0 on aggregate. In the next round, the Blues faced the formidable Czech side Dukla Prague. They won the first leg at Goodison 2–1 but lost 1–0 in the Czech capital to go out on the away goals rule. The club qualified again in 1979–80 but made an early exit at the hands of Feyenoord, the Dutch club winning both games 1–0.

UNDEFEATED. Everton have remained undefeated at home throughout just one Football League season – 1962–63, when they won 14 and drew seven of their 21 home matches to win the first division championship, setting a new club record points total of 61. The Blues' longest run of undefeated Football League matches home and away, is 20 between 29 April 1978 and 16 December 1978. Everton's best and longest undefeated home sequence in the Football League is of 39 matches between 16 September 1961 and 7 September 1963, coming to an end when the Blues lost 4–3 to Burnley.

UNDERSOIL HEATING. Underground heating wires were installed at Everton's pre-war practice ground in 1937 in an area behind the

Stanley Park goal. During the war, the area was used as a barrage balloon site. Army engineers ripped the heating system to shreds when they laid a concrete base. In the 1970s, an asphalt surface was put down to create the Everton car park. In May 1958, Everton became the first club to experiment with undersoil heating when electrical wiring was first installed at Goodison at a cost of £16,000. Ultimately, it was discovered that the drains could not cope with the melted ice and snow. The pitch had to be dug up and new drains laid. Further attempts at undersoil heating were tried and abandoned before the present system, which is one of the finest in the country, was introduced.

UNSWORTH, DAVID. David Unsworth made his Football League debut for Everton while still a trainee at Tottenham Hotspur on 25 April 1992. Although substituting at left-back for Andy Hinchcliffe, he scored a stunning equalising goal with a first-touch volley from a corner in a 3–3 thriller. He began his career as a left-back but Everton manager Mike Walker switched him to central defence at the start of the 1994–95 campaign. England manager Terry Venables called him into his Umbro Cup squad after a commanding FA Cup final performance alongside Dave Watson. He made his full international debut in the 2–1 win over Japan in June 1995. He was voted the club's Player of the Season. He continued to improve over the next two seasons even though he failed to add to his full England cap, but in the summer of 1997, after playing in 130 league and Cup games for the Blues, he left Goodison to join West Ham United, later returning to join The Blues after a very short stay at Villa Park.

UNUSUAL GOALS. During the league match between Tottenham Hotspur and Everton at White Hart Lane on 12 April 1924, which the Blues won 5–2, Sam Chedgzoy wrote himself into the record books when he took a corner and dribbled the ball past bemused defenders and straight into the goal. Chedgzoy was an intelligent man and having carefully studied the rules of the game he realised that there was a loophole. So as an experiment, and as part of a bet, he decided to test the referee and the rulebook. The referee's first reaction was to disallow the goal, but it was eventually allowed to stand because at that time no rule had been infringed. The present rule, that a player taking a corner-kick must not be allowed to play the ball twice, was introduced later. On 23 November 1996, with the Leicester City players still protesting about the referee's decision to award a free-kick against them, Everton's Nick Barmby snatched the ball out of Kasey Keller's hands and quickly placed it for Andy Hinchcliffe to strike the ball into an empty net.

David Unsworth

UTILITY PLAYERS. A utility player is one of those particularly gifted footballers who can play in a number of different positions. One of Everton's earliest utility players was Jack Taylor, who nearly always gave a good account of himself in almost any position. An inspirational footballer, he could coax the very best out of those around him. Jackie Grant was another fine utility player who played in no fewer than seven different positions during his Goodison career, although he was a first-team regular for just one season, 1950–51, when he was ever-present. When Brian Harris joined Everton he was a winger but his classy play and subtle skills meant that he was able to adapt to almost every position. In his 12 seasons with the Goodison Park club, he played in every position for the first team except goalkeeper. Alex 'Sandy' Brown was brought to Goodison Park in the wake of the club's 1962–63 championship win. Brown was a real utility man, a defender who could move forward to stamp his authority on midfield. The Scotsman could even play in goal and his versatility led to him being named substitute for no fewer than 33 league games. Towards the end of the 1960s, players were encouraged to become more adaptable and see their roles as less stereotyped. However, at the same time, much less attention came to be paid to the implication of wearing a certain numbered shirt and so some of the more versatile players came to wear almost all the different numbered shirts at some stage or another, although this did not necessarily indicate a vast variety of positions. One such player was Alan Harper – a model professional who approached any task with enthusiasm and commitment. He had to learn to live with the tag of 'utility player' and, in a career of 227 games for the Goodison club, wore eight different numbered outfield shirts.

V

VAN DEN HAUWE, PAT. An uncompromising, hard-tackling defender, Pat Van Den Hauwe started his football career with Birmingham City. His progress was not helped by being called upon to alternate between full-back and central defence in a St Andrews side continually struggling against the drop. Eventually settling at left-back in 1983–84, he was too good a player for second division football when the Midlands outfit were relegated at the end of that campaign, and in September 1984 he joined Everton for £100,000. By the end of his first season at Goodison, he had helped Everton to win the Football League title and the European Cup-Winners' Cup, and to reach the FA Cup final, and he had won his first international cap. Although born in Belgium, where his father Rene had been a professional goalkeeper, he had opted out of National Service and was therefore ineligible to play for his country of birth. Instead he chose to play for Wales and made his debut against Spain in April 1985. Over the next four years he was a regular in the Everton sides which won the league title again in 1987 and reached the FA Cup finals in 1986 and 1989. He had played in 190 league and Cup games for the Blues by August 1989 when he moved to Tottenham Hotspur for a fee of £575,000. He finally collected an FA Cup winners' medal in May 1991 when Spurs beat Nottingham Forest, and went on to play in 140 first-team games for the White Hart Lane club before ending his career with Millwall.

VARADI, IMRE. London-born of Hungarian parents, Imre Varadi was working as an asphalter when he was sacked by non-league Letchworth Town. Playing Sunday league football, he was spotted by Sheffield

Pat Van Den Hauwe

United, whose manager Harry Haslam immediately offered him terms. He had played in only ten league games when Everton boss Gordon Lee paid £80,000 for his services. He made his first-team debut as a substitute coming on for John Barton in a 2–1 defeat at Coventry City in October 1979. During his stay at Goodison, Varadi proved to be somewhat erratic, though his turn of speed and explosive shot brought him seven goals in 34 league and Cup appearances for the club. The most important of these strikes was Everton's second in a 2–1 FA Cup win over Liverpool in January 1981. At the end of that season, Varadi almost joined Benfica but on becoming a free agent, he signed for Newcastle United for £125,000. He went on to play for Sheffield Wednesday and West Bromwich Albion before returning to the north-west to join Manchester City. Later, he had a second spell with Sheffield Wednesday and then played for Leeds United, Rotherham United and Mansfield Town before ending his career with Scunthorpe United.

Roy Vernon

VERNON, ROY. Welsh international Roy Vernon had the chance to come to Goodison Park as a schoolboy but he turned down the opportunity and eventually turned professional with Blackburn Rovers. He won his first nine international caps as a Rovers player and, although he didn't realise it at the time, he robbed himself of a Wembley appearance when he finally became an Everton player in February 1960. It was Johnny Carey, his former manager at Blackburn, who lured him to Goodison in a £27,000 deal which took Eddie Thomas to Ewood Park in part-exchange. He made his Everton debut in a 2–0 home defeat by Wolverhampton Wanderers and went on to score nine goals in the last 12 games of the season. In 1960–61, he was the club's top scorer with 21 goals, including a hat-trick in a 4–1 win over Arsenal on the final day of the season. In 1961–62, he was again the club's top scorer with 26 goals in 37 league appearances, including another hat-trick in an 8–3 home win over Cardiff City. Vernon set about his work with compelling efficiency and skippered the side to the league title in 1962–63, netting a hat-trick in the 4–1 win over Fulham as the Blues clinched the championship. There were occasional brushes with Carey's successor, Harry Catterick, who made Vernon captain in the hope that the responsibility would mellow and mature the tempestuous Welshman. He added 13 more Welsh caps to his collection whilst with the Blues and when he moved to Stoke City in March 1965 he could look back on a record of 110 goals in 199 league and Cup games for the club. He eventually won 32 Welsh caps and when he lost his place in the Stoke side after five productive years with the Potters he moved to Halifax Town, where he ended his league career.

VICTORIES IN A SEASON – HIGHEST. In the 1969–70 season, Everton won 29 of their 42 league fixtures, the highest number of wins in the club's history, and took the league championship.

VICTORIES IN A SEASON – LOWEST. Everton's poorest performances came in seasons 1888–89, 1971–72 and 1979–80 when they won only nine matches. However, in 1888–89, the first season of the Football League, the Blues played only 22 matches. In seasons 1971–72 and 1979–80, the club played 42 matches. Despite their poor form, they were not relegated, finishing 15th and 19th respectively.

VIRR, ALBERT. Local-born Albert Virr was a tough-tackling half-back who made his Everton debut in a 1–0 home win over Tottenham Hotspur in January 1925. However, it was 1926–27 before he established himself as a regular in the Everton side. The following season, he proved himself to be a vital member of the club's championship-winning side, missing just three games. During the Blues' 2–0 FA Cup defeat at Chelsea in January 1929, he suffered a serious knee injury and although he attempted a comeback the following season the damage to the cartilage was so severe he had to retire.

WAINWRIGHT, EDDIE. Spotted playing for High Park in the Southport Amateur League, Eddie Wainwright joined Everton as an amateur in 1939. In his early days with the club, he was loaned out to Fleetwood in an effort to aid his development. During the war, Wainwright played representative football for the army and his goalscoring achievements forced Everton into giving him his first-team debut. Playing alongside Tommy Lawton and Joe Mercer, he was in the Everton side that went down 4–1 to Manchester United on 11 September 1943. A week later, he scored one of the Blues' goals in the return match as they beat United 6–1. He played in 66 wartime games for Everton, scoring 36 goals including hat-tricks against Stoke City (home 6–1) and Blackpool (home 7–1) in 1945–46. Making his league debut at home to Brentford on the opening day of the 1946–47 season, Wainwright scored a hat-trick in a 4–2 win over Sunderland at Goodison Park on 15 February 1947. In 1948–49, he hit four goals in a 5–0 home win over Blackpool and in 1949–50 was the club's leading scorer, hitting another three goals in a 3–0 win over Huddersfield Town, and scoring some important goals in the club's run to the semi-finals of the FA Cup. At the end of that season, he toured the USA and Canada with an FA party and later represented the Football League. He scored 76 goals in 228 league and Cup games for Everton before moving to Spotland to play for Rochdale.

WALKER, MIKE. Mike Walker arrived from Norwich City in January 1994, where he had been in the middle of contract negotiations, and Everton were later penalised by the Football League for poaching. The

Everton manager's first game produced a worrying 1–1 draw at Bolton in the FA Cup but his first league game in charge seemed to herald a new era as Swindon Town were beaten 6–2 at Goodison. However, the new mood of optimism was short-lived as the Blues crashed out of the FA Cup at home to Bolton just four days later. With Bill Kenwright and Peter Johnson bidding to take control of the club, there was little money to spend on new players and the Blues had to rely on Graham Stuart's winner in the final game of the season to keep them in the top flight. With Peter Johnson successfully gaining control of the club, Walker was able to strengthen his squad for the 1994–95 season by spending £3 million on Nigerian World Cup star Daniel Amokachi. However, the club's results continued to be disappointing and in November 1994 he was dismissed. In June 1996, Walker returned to Carrow Road to take charge of Norwich City for a second time before resigning in April 1998.

WARTIME FOOTBALL. In spite of the outbreak of the First World War in 1914, the major football leagues embarked upon their planned programme of matches for the ensuing season and these were completed on schedule at the end of April the following year when the Blues won the first division championship. With the season barely over, the Football League announced what had long been expected – that there would be no more league football until hostilities ceased. In place of the league system, an ad hoc Lancashire League was established but many of the regular players were absent, either serving abroad or finding alternative employment to aid the war effort. Goodison Park was used for army drill and there was even a baseball match between Chicago Giants and New York Whitesox. During the war, the club contributed £500 to the War Fund and organised regular collections at games. Even the players dug into their pockets, giving a weekly remittance to the fund, and they received training in case they were called upon to serve on the front. In complete contrast to the events of 1914, once war was declared on 3 September 1939, the Football League programme of 1939–40 was suspended and for a while there was no football of any description. In October 1939, the game continued on a regional basis and, with many of the younger players already enlisting in the services, it was agreed that a guest system would be allowed. Even so, some of the opposition was ridiculously weak for a team like Everton and they won 9–2 at Tranmere and 7–0 at home to Stockport County. The league was extended for the 1940–41 season, Everton finishing fifth. Not all teams played an equal number of fixtures and positions were determined on goal average. The next

Dave Watson

season became even more complicated, being split into two parts. The Blues were heavily beaten 8–3 at Stoke City in their opening fixture, but did beat Manchester City 9–0. In the second part of the season, they fared even worse, losing 11–1 at Wolverhampton Wanderers. The next three seasons were similar, with none of the matches being taken too seriously. Goodison Park inevitably suffered during the German air raids on the city of Liverpool. The club received £5,000 from the War Damage Commission for essential repair work.

WATSON, DAVE. Dave Watson started his career at Anfield. However, the consistency of central defenders Alan Hansen and Phil Thompson meant he failed to break into the first team and he moved to Norwich

City for a fee of £50,000, plus another £50,000 after 25 appearances. This fee was to be doubled if he won an England cap, which he did in the summer of 1984 in the historic win over Brazil. A stalwart in the heart of the Canaries' defence, Watson topped 40 appearances in each of his last five years with the club, scoring some important goals. Everton had wanted him in the summer of 1985 but had to wait another year before getting their man. Derek Mountfield contracted a long-term injury and so Howard Kendall moved to cover the gap, signing Watson for £900,000. He was by now a known quantity, having appeared in 256 first-team games for the Carrow Road club and proved himself an inspiring leader from the back. He made his Everton debut in a 2–0 home win over Nottingham Forest on the opening day of the 1986–87 season and soon formed a very effective central defensive partnership with Kevin Ratcliffe, which lasted until 1991 when the Welshman gave way to Martin Keown. In his first season at Goodison, Watson helped the Blues to their second league championship in three years and also won an FA Cup finalists' medal in 1989 when Everton went down to Liverpool. Having assumed the captaincy in succession to Kevin Ratcliffe in 1992, he led the Blues to their FA Cup success in 1995 and was voted Man of the Match against Manchester United. Now approaching his 37th birthday, he has appeared in over 450 first-team games and remains vital to the club's cause.

WATSON, TOMMY. One of the club's great servants, Tommy Watson joined Everton from Blyth Spartans in his native north-east. Quickly impressing with his tough tackling and close control, he made his first-team debut in a 2–2 draw at Brentford in January 1937. The following season he scored his only goal for the club as Blackpool were beaten 3–1 and in 1938–39 he appeared in 16 of Everton's championship-winning games. For most of the club's other games that season, Watson was 12th man and his team-mates clubbed together to buy him a special cushion so that he would be more comfortable sitting on the trainer's bench. During the war, he played in 190 games for Everton including one in goal in a 2–1 defeat at Tranmere Rovers on Boxing Day 1942. He continued to play for the club after the hostilities, before being appointed first-team trainer. In 1968 he joined the club's promotions department, later working as a part-time barman at the 300 Club.

WEST, GORDON. Goalkeeper Gordon West made his league debut with first division Blackpool as a 17-year-old in 1961, temporarily replacing Tony Waiters. In March 1962, Harry Catterick paid £27,000

Gordon West

to secure the services of West, his first signing as Everton boss. It was then a record fee for a goalkeeper, and it paid immediate dividends as West replaced Albert Dunlop and helped the Blues take the league championship in his first full season. West was an instinctive performer and courageous at close-quarter blocks; he was also breathtaking as a shot-stopper. One weakness that the Everton goalkeeper did possess was a rather inadequate kick – a legacy of a long-standing thigh injury – but the big keeper compensated amply with constructive throws in the manner of Manchester City's Bert Trautmann. For the first two seasons following his debut against Wolverhampton Wanderers, which the Blues won 4–0, he shared the goalkeeping duties with Andy Rankin. After that, he missed only a handful of games and picked up a second championship medal in 1969–70. West endeared himself to the Kopites after reacting to one of their customary fusillades of abuse by blowing them a kiss; their response was to present him with a handbag! Yet despite his ebullient personality, Gordon West was notoriously nervous before a game. After playing in 399 league and Cup games for the Goodison club, Gordon West left Everton at the end of the 1972–73 season, having won three England caps – there might have been more but for his withdrawal for family reasons. He was lured back to the game two years later by neighbouring Tranmere Rovers. Meanwhile, Everton were not to find a truly satisfactory replacement for West until the arrival of Neville Southall.

WHITE, TOMMY. Having joined Everton from Southport in 1927, Tommy White made his debut as a deputy for Dixie Dean, scoring two goals in a 7–0 win over West Ham United. It was his only game that season but in 1928–29 he began to establish himself in the Blues' first team. Although he could play in a variety of positions, he had been bought as a goalscorer. He scored his first hat-trick for the club on the final day of Everton's relegation season of 1929–30 as Sunderland were beaten 4–1. The following season, he found his appearances restricted but still managed to score a goal a game in his ten outings as the Blues won the second division championship. His best season in terms of goals scored was 1931–32 when he netted 18 in 23 games, including all three in the 3–0 victory over Portsmouth, as the club won the league championship. In 1933 he played centre-half for England against Italy in Rome. It was a position he had played as a schoolboy and one that he reverted to at club level towards the end of his Everton career. In 1937, having scored 66 goals in 202 games, he left Goodison to end his career with Northampton Town.

WHITTLE, ALAN. Despite helping Everton beat West Bromwich Albion 6–2 on his debut in March 1968, Alan Whittle's inconsistency meant that he often found himself on the sidelines. However, he won a league championship medal in 1969–70, scoring 11 goals in 15 games, and appeared in more than half of the club's games the following season. In December 1972, after he had scored 26 goals in 89 first-team games, he left Goodison to join Crystal Palace for a fee of £100,000. He scored 19 goals in 108 league games for the Selhurst Park club, later playing for Leyton Orient and Bournemouth before trying his luck in Iran.

WILLIAMS, BEN. Born in Penhriwceber in South Wales, Ben Williams seriously considered a career in boxing before Swansea Town offered him the chance to turn professional in 1923. The strong-tackling full-back made 97 appearances for the Swans before signing for Everton in December 1929. After making his debut in a 4–0 win over Derby County, Williams began to form an outstanding full-back partnership with Warney Cresswell. He captained the Toffees to the second division championship in 1930–31 and at the end of the season won the first of his ten caps for Wales when he played against Northern Ireland. Injured during Everton's 5–1 win over Wolverhampton Wanderers on 24 December 1932, he underwent a cartilage operation from which he never fully recovered. In 1936, he joined Newport County and later was appointed club coach at Somerton Park.

WILSON, RAY. Widely regarded as the best left-back in European football when he won a World Cup winners' medal with England in 1966, Ray Wilson joined Everton in the summer of 1964 from Huddersfield Town. He had been at Leeds Road for 13 years and made 266 league appearances for the Yorkshire club. He made his Everton debut in a 2–0 win at Stoke City on the opening day of the 1964–65 season and over the next four seasons he went on to appear in 153 league and Cup games for the Blues. He had missed a number of games through injury but after damaging a knee in training, he required surgery and was never quite the same player afterwards. Having made 63 appearances for England, he was rather surprisingly given a free transfer by Everton, making him an attractive proposition for a number of clubs. He joined Oldham Athletic in 1969 before moving to Bradford City as player-coach.

WOLSTENHOLME, SAM. Born at Little Lever near Bolton, wing-half Sam Wolstenholme joined Everton towards the end of 1897 and made his debut in a 1–1 draw at home to Stoke on 17 January 1898. It was his only game for the club that season but midway through the 1898–99 campaign he forced his way into the side and stayed there for the next three seasons. In 1900–1 he was an ever-present but at the end of the 1903–4 season, he was surprisingly allowed to sign for Blackburn Rovers. Still only 25 years of age, he had the previous month made his international debut against Scotland and whilst at Ewood Park added to his collection of international caps. Though he may have looked past his best with his balding pate and bandy legs, he went on to give Rovers four years' good service before joining Croydon Common. After helping them out of the Southern League, he joined Norwich City before hanging up his boots.

George Wood

WOOD, GEORGE. Goalkeeper George Wood joined Blackpool during the 1971–72 season from East Stirling and went on to appear in 117 league games for the Bloomfield Road club before joining Everton for £150,000 in August 1977. An ever-present in his first two seasons with the club, he went on to appear in 114 consecutive league and Cup games after making his debut in a 3–1 home defeat by Nottingham Forest on 20 August 1977. He kept 19 clean sheets in 1977–78 and 15 in 1978–79, this form helping him win two Scottish caps whilst with the club. However, midway through the 1979–80 season, the inconsistency that had plagued the early part of his career returned and he lost his place to Martin Hodge. He did play in the final four games of the season, conceding just one goal, but in the close season he was allowed to join Arsenal for £150,000. In three seasons at Highbury he made 60 league appearances before leaving to play for Crystal Palace. He made over 200 first-team appearances for the Selhurst Park club before playing for Cardiff City and later Hereford United.

WORST START. The club's worst-ever start to a season was in 1994–95. It took 13 league games to record the first victory of the season, drawing four and losing eight of the opening fixtures. The run ended with a 1–0 win over West Ham United at Goodison Park on 1 November 1994. After drawing their next match, the Blues won three consecutive matches and were unbeaten in the last seven games of the season to finish 15th. In 1958–59, the club lost their first six matches of the season, scoring just four goals, yet conceding 20. Later that season, they lost 10–4 at Tottenham Hotspur but managed to end the campaign in 16th place.

WRIGHT, BILLY. A life-long Everton supporter, Billy Wright made his debut for the Goodison club as a substitute for George Telfer in a 2–0 home win over Leicester City in February 1978. By the start of the following season, the hard-working defender had established himself in the heart of the Everton defence and was later made club captain. The popular Wright began to put on weight and just hours before a league game at Ipswich Town on 11 December 1982, manager Howard Kendall told his captain he was being left out as a disciplinary measure for weighing 8lbs more than the club allowed! He never played for the Blues again and six months later, after 198 league and Cup games, he joined Birmingham City on a free transfer. Although the club were relegated in his first season at St Andrews, he helped them back to the first division in 1984–85.

WRIGHT, TOMMY. A former England Schoolboy international, Tommy Wright joined Everton as an inside-forward before being converted to wing-half and then right-back. He made his first-team debut in a 1–1 draw at Blackpool in October 1964 as a replacement for Scottish international Alex Parker. A virtual ever-present over the next nine seasons, he won an FA Cup winners' medal in 1966 as the Blues beat Sheffield Wednesday 3–2 in the final. In 1968, he won the first of 11 full international caps for England when he played against Russia in the European Championship third-place play-off. He also represented England in the 1970 World Cup finals in Mexico. Tommy Wright was one of the most constructive back-four players in British football and liked nothing better than to force his way down the flanks when the opportunity arose. In 1969–70, when Everton won the league championship, Wright was one of four ever-presents and in the game against Nottingham Forest scored the only goal of the game to give the Blues two vital points. One of football's natural gentlemen, he went on to play in 371 league and Cup games for Everton.

X

X. In football 'X' traditionally stands for a draw. The club record for the number of draws in a season is 18. In 1925–26, 1971–72 and 1974–75 they managed 18 draws out of 42 matches.

XMAS DAY. There was a time when football matches were regularly played on Christmas Day, but in recent years the game's authorities have dropped the fixture from the calendar. In the club's first Football League match to be played on Christmas Day, they went down 4–0 at home to Sunderland. In seasons 1905–6 and 1906–7, Everton travelled to Bury, losing 3–2 and winning 2–1 respectively. On each occasion, Everton's goals were scored by Sharp and Young. On Christmas Day 1926, Dixie Dean scored four of Everton's goals in a 5–4 win over Sunderland. The Roker Park side were beaten 6–2 in 1934, and two years later Derby County were defeated 7–0 with Jimmy Cunliffe netting a hat-trick. During the war years, Everton played Liverpool at Anfield on Christmas Day 1940 and lost 3–1. In 1942–43 and 1943–44, Everton's Christmas Day fixture paired them with Manchester City. England centre-forward Tommy Lawton scored a hat-trick in each fixture as Everton won 6–3 at Goodison Park in 1942 and 5–3 at Maine Road in 1943. The last time Everton played on Christmas Day was in 1957 when a George Kirby goal gave them a share of the spoils in a 1–1 draw at home to Bolton Wanderers.

Y

YOUNG, ALEX. One of the most talked about players of his generation, Alex Young arrived at Goodison Park in November 1960 along with Hearts colleague George Thomson. He didn't make his Everton debut until 17 December against Tottenham Hotspur because he arrived on Merseyside carrying a knee injury sustained in playing for the British Army. He wasn't a powerhouse Number 9 in the tradition of Dixie Dean and Tommy Lawton, but Alex Young was majestic in the air. His timing was exquisite, so much so that he seemed to hover, a talent never better illustrated than by his near-post header past Bill Brown in the crucial 1–0 victory over Spurs at Goodison in April 1963 during the club's title run-in. During that season, he scored 22 goals and laid on many more for Roy Vernon. Young seemed to have plenty of time. He knew instinctively where to play the ball and was always well aware of all the options open to him without looking up. To go with his flair and grace, Young possessed a vicious shot as well as good heading ability. Surprisingly, for all his skill and natural ability, Young played for Scotland on only eight occasions, the first against England in 1960 whilst still with Hearts. His blond hair made him a distinctive figure on the field of play and the fans called him the 'Golden Vision' – an inspired nickname which was also the title of a television play about Evertonians in general and the popular Scotsman in particular. In August 1968, Alex Young, who had scored 87 goals in 271 league and Cup games for the Blues, became player-manager of Glentoran. However, after only two months he joined Stockport County. Unfortunately, he was forced to retire with knee trouble, having played only 23 games for the Edgeley Park club.

Alex Young

YOUNG, ALEX 'SANDY'. The first of two Scots strikers to share this name, this Alex Young was better known as 'Sandy' and, like his namesake, became a proven goalscorer. His career took him to St Mirren and Falkirk before he joined Everton in the summer of 1901. He made his debut in a 1–1 draw at Aston Villa and over the next ten seasons went on to score 125 goals in 314 league and Cup outings. In 1906, Young was the man who scored the 75th-minute goal which won the FA Cup for the club in the match against Newcastle United as he converted a cross from Jack Sharp. His best season in terms of goals scored was 1906–07 when he netted 28 goals in 33 league games including four in a 9–1 win against Manchester City. He had already produced one of the best individual performances of the Merseyside derby when he scored four goals in a 5–2 home win over Liverpool on 1 April 1904. After helping the Blues to fourth position in the first division in 1910–11, the Scottish international, who won two caps whilst with Everton, moved to Tottenham Hotspur. He started well with three goals in his first two games but failed to score in the next three and was left out of the team. He returned north to finish the season with Manchester City and then had a year with South Liverpool before emigrating to Australia in 1914.

YOUNGEST PLAYER. The youngest player to appear in a first-class fixture for Everton is Joe Royle who played in the first division match against Blackpool (away 0–2) on 15 January 1966 when he was 16 years 288 days old.

YOUTH CUP. Everton have reached the final of the FA Youth Cup on five occasions. They were two-legged affairs and the aggregate scores are:

1961	Chelsea 5	Everton 3
1965	Everton 3	Arsenal 2
1977	Crystal Palace 1	Everton 0
1983	Norwich City 6	Everton 5 (including replay)
1984	Everton 4	Stoke City 2

Z

ZENITH. Few fans will argue over which moments have been the finest in the club's history. In 1984–85, Everton won the Canon League championship and the European Cup-Winners' Cup after beating Rapid Vienna in the final in Rotterdam. The club also lost to Manchester United in the FA Cup final at Wembley, ending hopes of achieving what would have been an astonishing treble.

ZENITH DATA SYSTEMS CUP. The Zenith Data Systems Cup replaced the Simod Cup from the 1989–90 season but the Blues didn't enter the competition, waiting until the following season before getting involved. In their first match, Dave Watson scored two goals as Blackburn Rovers were beaten 4–1 at Ewood Park. The Blues repeated the scoreline in the next round at home to Sunderland with ace marksman Tony Cottee grabbing all four goals. It was the former West Ham forward who scored the only goal of the next round tie at Oakwell against Barnsley. In the first leg of the Northern final, the Blues drew 3–3 with Leeds United at Elland Road before winning 3–1 after extra-time in the second leg at Goodison Park. In the final, however, they lost 4–1 to Crystal Palace with Everton's goal being scored by Robert Warzycha. In 1991–92, the Blues beat Oldham Athletic 3–2 but then lost 2–1 at Leicester City in what proved to be their last game in the competition.